THE SEARCH
FOR THE
EARLY CHURCH

THE SEARCH FOR THE EARLY CHURCH

NEW TESTAMENT PRINCIPLES FOR TODAY'S CHURCH

WILLIAM STEUART McBIRNIE

B.A., B.D., M.R.E., D.R.E., Ph.D., D.D., F.R.G.S., Th.D., L.H.D., O.S.J.

TYNDALE HOUSE PUBLISHERS, INC.

WHEATON, ILLINOIS

All biblical quotations used in this book are taken from the King James Version, unless otherwise noted.

Library of Congress Catalog Card Number 78-55982
ISBN 0-8423-5834-X
Copyright © 1978 by Tyndale House Publishers,
    Inc., Wheaton, Illinois.
First printing, September 1978.
Printed in the United States of America.

Contents

Part One
CHURCHES OF THE NEW TESTAMENT ERA: PRINCIPLES

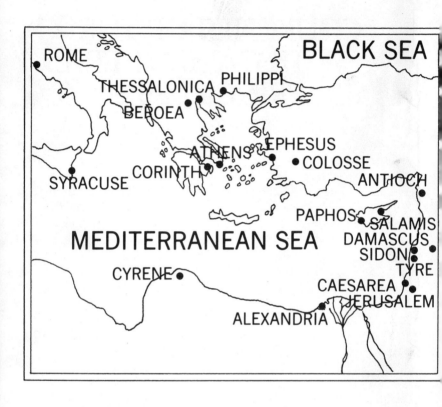

Churches established during first years of Christianity, except in Asia Minor.

Introduction
WELCOME TO THE WORLD OF THE EARLY CHURCH!

When I was a very young preacher, I heard a minister describe what he termed, "the imperative for the church today to get back to the New Testament church." This meant to me then, "Let's get back to the Bible; let's return to the *doctrines* of the Apostles and renounce unscriptural beliefs."

The supposition that the term "New Testament church" was another name for early Christianity-in-general seemed sufficient at the time. Indeed, is this not the concept held today by most evangelicals? At any rate, at that time to this writer, the word *church* meant Christianity itself, the source of doctrine; not primarily the congregation.

As a result of years of university and seminary work, majoring in church history while earning three doctorates, and doing a great deal of field survey of early Christian archaeology, further questions have had to be faced. Can we "*get back* to the New Testament" in doctrine without also recovering the principles of the operation of the New Testament era *congregations*? What exactly was a "New Testament church?" Is it really important to us today?

Since the first century, the world has advanced, so that we have many tools and methods unknown to the Apostles. Can we use them in the church today and still retain the power of early Christianity? On another level, has there been further revelation about the intentions of God for the church since the close of the New Testament era? What must a contemporary congregation do in order to become like the churches founded by the Apostles? Has the world changed so much that being like the early churches would be a step backwards? Has the church the authority and right to change? If so, how is such change to be effected?

9

ATTEMPTS TO RECOVER THE NATURE OF EARLY CHRISTIANITY

Church history is replete with examples of Christians who at various times have tried to copy the early church. In the last century, they were a part of what has become known as "the restoration movement." Countless churches have been organized to copy some particular aspect of primitive or early church practice.

The Quakers in their worship services practiced being led by the Spirit, as was stressed in the Corinthian church. The Baptists have administered "believers' baptism" only, as did all the churches of the New Testament era. The Christian (Disciples) Church has followed the quest for a rational faith in the spirit of unity, as did the church at Berea. Pietists of many denominations have looked primarily for deeper spiritual experience, as did the church at Caesarea. The Reformation churches (Presbyterian, Reformed, and others) have attempted to recover the orderly, organized church of Jerusalem. We honor all sincere attempts to recover the early church, even when they are partial.

WHY MANY HAVE FAILED

It is evident that these movements, which attempted the conscious imitation of *some* aspects of the early churches, have all failed in *other* measures to reflect the *complete* organization, program, and policy of the New Testament era churches founded by the Apostles. This is not an accusation, but an observation.

To fail to copy the whole by emphasizing only a part may be the result of either failing to grasp what the early churches believed and practiced, or of deliberately ignoring the nature of the church in its primitive (i.e., earliest, hence purest) pattern.

ESSENTIAL MARKS OF THE EARLY CHURCHES

If a particular church desires to be a "New Testament church," it would need to follow positive historical examples in each of these areas: *piety, program, policy,* and *power.* For a

Welcome to the World of the Early Church!

church to duplicate the early church in only one or two of these areas is not enough to qualify it as a contemporary version of a "New Testament church."

For example: Denominations were unknown to the Christians of the first century. There is a serious question as to whether a denomination can accurately be called a "church." The word *church* (*ekklesia*) to the Apostles meant a congregation.

The concept of catholicity (universality of organization) came much later. Never, for instance, did the Apostles use the so-called Apostles' Creed, which was a product of the second or third century. While there may have been certain creedal statements embedded in the text of the New Testament, it is certain that none was ever worded, "I believe in the holy *catholic* church." Such a concept was foreign to the early congregations, each of which was autonomous in government. Our concept of the church is therefore limited to the congregation, not Christianity at large.

This is not necessarily criticism of churches or denominations. It is to say, however, that if a congregation seeks at least to resemble the New Testament era churches, it may have to reappraise some cherished practices. It might have to study the principles of the local church in the New Testament era.

Can a church today have power as the early churches did, and yet reject the programs, policies (i.e., doctrines), and purposes of those churches? Our Lord surely must have known what He was doing when He taught the disciples how to found and organize churches as well as to win individuals.

This writer's aim is not to awaken old quarrels. Nor is it to deny that programs, methods, and means have indeed changed for the better in some instances. Undoubtedly, many things which were added to the New Testament concept of the nature and purpose of the local church have practical value. But, we ask, is it not likely that at least *some* of our historical and modern "improvements" are not improvements at all, but distractions? How shall we know unless we first learn what the primitive churches were like, for comparison or contrast?

We further ask: Is it not possible that the modern church has much to learn from the early churches, since they were closer to our Lord in time and location than are we? If so, then should we not take a more careful look at the early churches? Should

11

we not be sure the impressions and conclusions we have held hitherto are accurate? Those are the questions faced in this study.

THE PLAN OF THE BOOK

This volume is the third of a trilogy. The first, *The Search for the Twelve Apostles* (Tyndale House, Wheaton, Ill., 1973), is an attempt to gather every known fact (beyond the biblical record) about the twelve men Jesus chose.

The second book, *The Search for the Authentic Tomb of Jesus* (Acclaimed Books, Montrose, Cal., 1975), is the first full-length book on that subject and explores the different theories of the places of the crucifixion and entombment of Jesus. It has perhaps brought to light some heretofore unknown facts about the "historical Jesus."

This third volume, *The Search for the Early Church*, endeavors to look at thirteen major cities featured in the New Testament story of the expansion of Christianity, in order to draw out some of the universal and timeless *principles* which came out of the confrontation of the Gospel with the culture of the first century. We will not deal at length with the various *doctrines* of the New Testament as such, for that subject has been well covered by others. Our main concern will be with the early churches as organizations.

The author's book on the Apostles was written for scholars, but it was hoped that laymen would find many parts of it interesting and informative. The second book, about the place of the crucifixion and tomb of Jesus, was intended to help pilgrims traveling to the Holy Land explore intelligently the origins of the Christian faith. This third volume on the early churches is written for church leaders and church members, to set forth what the apostolic churches were like in organization, practices, programs, and purposes as congregations. We do not use the word *church* in any other sense in this book.

The world of the first century is this writer's second home. Jerusalem, Athens, Rome, and most of the lesser-known cities of the Bible have been visited by me again and again on some thirty-five journeys to the "lands of the Book." My search for

12

Welcome to the World of the Early Church!

the early church was given much impetus from the growing realization that the first century was not as different from ours as we may sometimes think. It is always a joy to walk in the familiar footsteps of Jesus and His followers, to enter ancient, long-buried cities and houses, to experience what the total life of people in biblical times was like.

Perhaps something of that experience may here be conveyed to the reader. *Welcome to the world of the early church!*

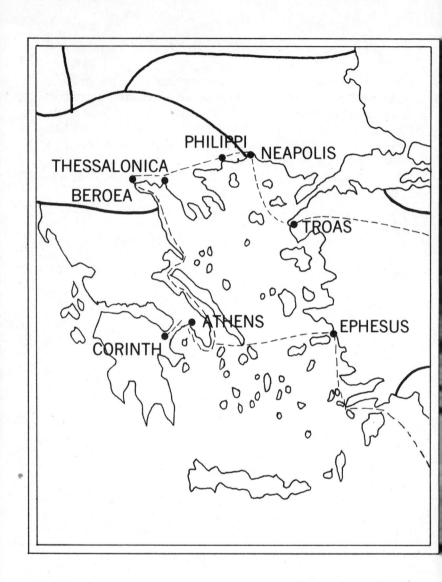

St. Paul in Greece; the second journey.

One
THE SEARCH FOR
THE EARLY CHURCH

By "early church," we mean the primitive or first-century, local apostolic church (or congregation) wherever it was found. Why should contemporary Christians care about it enough to search for it? Does such a search for something so ancient have any real relevancy for the individual believer today? Does an institution long buried in history have a boon to bestow upon today's Christianity?

OUR SOURCES OF INFORMATION

Where shall we search? Most obviously, the richest sources are the New Testament and to a limited degree early Christian history (some of which is in the New Testament itself). We must peel back, when possible, all the layers of customs and beliefs which were added during the centuries since apostolic times. We must examine those practices and forms which may or may not have added to Christianity as it was found in its primitive, and hence uncorrupted, form.

Perhaps we may also gain from a fresh look at the Book of Acts and the events which occurred in the cities featured in it so prominently. It could be that there is a yet unemphasized and very instructive outline in the Book of Acts involving principles which brought the growth of authentic, original Christianity.

So far as we are able to tell, people themselves have not changed in the centuries since the Apostles, even though our technology and world view have been greatly expanded. We who are Christians today are convinced that real Christianity still fits all people. Especially is this true since Christ is the eternal Son of God and the final revelation of the will and truth

15

of God. He said He was "the way, the truth, and the life." One must believe *that* or one is not a genuine Christian in the historic sense.

The question is, How much can today's church add to or take away from the original belief and practice without being distorted out of the shape that Jesus and the Apostles intended it to have? Jude's memorable phrase (in the Greek) has to be confronted: "the faith *once for all* delivered unto the saints" (vs. 3). If "the faith" has been delivered "once for all," then it dare not be changed or added to, lest it become something less or something more than God meant it to be. That belief has long been held by most orthodox Christians as it applies to *doctrines* of the Faith.

In this book's quest, however, we seek not for doctrines, but for the fundamental and necessary church organizations and ecclesiastical practices of the early churches which matured during the apostolic age. Christianity had in those early days a dynamic power, which is still available to us today. It is not enough to say that this power was and is the Holy Spirit. We gladly acknowledge this. But the Holy Spirit in all ages is in confrontation with culture, philosophy, religion, human nature, customs, social behavior, and the secular state. It is the interaction of the Holy Spirit upon the Christian believer, in relationship with those other forces, which causes the church to be what it is in every age and every land.

The question is not, therefore, what has been the resultant church, but rather *what should it be*?

ATTEMPTS TO CORRUPT AND TO RESTORE PRIMITIVE CHRISTIANITY

Every revival of dynamic Christianity has been due to a rediscovery or reemphasis of the pure Christianity of the first century. Like a river which is pure at its source, Christianity flowed from Jesus Christ to the Apostles and from them to the first-century Christians. But it was barely underway when influences from other sources began to color the waters. The further from the Source the river flowed, the more it changed and the more polluted it became through these influences.

The Search for the Early Church

From time to time reformers have said, "Let's go back to the Source and begin anew." Often, however, they unconsciously carried some of the unchristian pollution of their churches back with them. Few were really objective; few could detach themselves from the strong and prejudiced personalities of leaders, the influence of existing culture, politics, or religious custom. Hence, most reformations or restoration movements have been only partial in their return to the Source. Frequently, compromise has seemed necessary. Whether or not it was really necessary is open to debate.

It is obvious that most denominations can trace their origins to the impact of unique racial, national, or leadership attitudes. Most meaningful denominational differences today are to be found in a divergence of opinion as to what "pure" Christianity is, or was. Few sincere Christians would simply write off "pure" Christianity or flatly reject it. Rather, they would say, "Our group has in fact returned to it, even though we may have admitted some features in our practice or beliefs which are different from those of early Christians. But in the main, we have indeed returned to the pure *substance* of what Jesus intended. The differences can be explained as peripheral or attributable to the fact that we live in a different time and face different circumstances than those existing in the first century."

Is this a valid position?

Those who say it is must face the question of whether they are merely rationalizing that which they find inconvenient to give up. Or they may not really know what New Testament era Christianity was. Indeed, *can* anyone really know what it was, and can the eternal principles Christ gave His Apostles be adapted to existing circumstances today without serious change or loss?

THE NEED FOR OBJECTIVITY

It is hard to rise up from one's religious milieu and see Christianity objectively. Christianity demands a certain personal commitment to Christ and the church. *Can* one ever critically examine or objectively analyze that to which one has given a wholehearted commitment? Admittedly it is difficult. However, this writer believes it can be done if one approaches the issue positively and constructively.

THE CHURCH AND THE FORCES WHICH CORRUPT IT

There seems to be a centrifugal force at work in Christianity, constantly in motion, taking the believer and his church away from Christ, the Apostles, and the teachings of the early churches as recorded in the New Testament. Often egotism on the part of leaders and the desire for novelty can cause this psychological and cultural phenomenon. This tendency is at work in every congregation, and in every Christian denomination.

To counter this tendency, if churches are to remain loyal to historic Christianity, they must return frequently and deliberately to the Source. Our churches must not remain primarily explainable in terms of any given culture. Ideally, they must rise above culture. To accomplish this, it is too simple a solution just to "go back to the Bible." We must ask, which translation of the Bible? What understanding or interpretation of it? What assistance is available to help us see the pattern for the church objectively? A tendency toward an oversimplification of the Bible is really not helpful.

If we are *unwilling* to engage in a rigorous study of church history, we are doomed not only to repeat the mistakes it records, but also never even to know what errors have been committed. We may pride ourselves that *our* faith, *our* church, *our* denomination is the one which is truly and wholly Christian. Never was there a more deceptive pride than that. We must face the questions of the intended nature and destiny of the church with open minds and a willingness to be shocked at discovering that this dreadful centrifugal force is secretly at work even in our own beloved church. "While we slept, an enemy came and sowed tares," reported the servants of the farmer in Jesus' parable. The "enemy" is still about, and his supply of tares is still ample.

About the year A.D. 200, Tertullian, an important post-apostolic figure, wrote as plain and as eloquent an explanation of the

18

need for churches to return to the Source, the Savior and His designated Apostles, as any we have:

> Hence then the ruling which we lay down; that since Jesus Christ sent out the Apostles to preach, no others are to be accepted as preachers but those whom Christ appointed.... Now the substance of their preaching, that is, Christ's revelation to them, must be approved, on my ruling, only through the testimony of those churches which the Apostles founded by preaching to them both *viva voce* and afterwards by their letters. If this is so, it is likewise clear that all doctrine which accords with these apostolic churches, the sources and origins of the faith, must be reckoned as truth, since it maintains without doubt what the churches received from the Apostles, the Apostles from Christ, and Christ from God.... We are in communion with the apostolic churches because there is no difference of doctrine. This is our guarantee of truth.
>
> Even if these heresies should devise such a pedigree, it will be no help to them. For their very teaching, when compared with that of the Apostles, will proclaim by its diversity and contrariety that it originates neither from an Apostle nor from an apostolic man; for the Apostles would not have diverged from one another in doctrine; no more would the apostolic man have put out teaching at variance with that of the Apostles.... This test will be applied to those churches of a later date, which are daily being founded. Though they cannot therefore produce an Apostle or an apostolic man for their founder, still, if they unite in holding the same faith, they equally are reckoned apostolic because of the kinship of their teaching. If it is agreed that what is earlier is truer, and what is there from the beginning is earlier, and that what issues from the Apostles is from the beginning, it will equally be agreed that what has been held sacred in the churches of the Apostles is that which has been handed down from the Apostles.

Churches of the New Testament Era: Principles

We are a body united by a common religious profession, by a godly discipline, by a bond of hope. We meet together as an assembly and congregation that as an organized force we may assail God with our prayers. Such violence is acceptable to God. We pray also for emperors, for their ministers, and those in authority, for man's temporal welfare, for the peace of the world, for the delay of the end of all things. We are compelled to refresh our memories of our sacred writings, if any special feature of the present time requires warning or reconsideration. In any case we nourish our faith with these holy utterances, we stimulate our hope, we establish our confidence; and at the same time we strengthen our discipline by the inculcation of the precepts. In the same place also exhortations, rebukes, and godly censures are administered. Each of us puts in a small donation on the appointed day in each month, or when he chooses, and only if he chooses, and only if he can; for no one is compelled and the offering is voluntary. This is as it were the deposit fund of kindness. For we do not pay our money from this fund to spend on feasts or drinking parties or inelegant "blowouts," but to pay for the nourishment and burial of the poor, to support boys and girls who are orphan and destitute; and old people who are confined to the house; and those who have been shipwrecked; and any who are in the mines, or banished to islands, or in prison, or are pensioners because of their confession, provided they are suffering because they belong to the followers of God.[1]

While we might not share the views of Tertullian about the violence of prayer and so on, he gives a general argument about the valid connection of the apostolic directions with the later churches which we can accept and value.

[1]Henry Bettenson, ed., *The Early Christian Fathers* (New York: Oxford University Press, 1969), n.p.

The Search for the Early Church

The apostolic congregations do not, because of the limited knowledge we have about them, tell us everything which goes to make up a perfect church. We must put all we learn from our sources—i.e., the entire teaching of the New Testament plus certain facts from early church history—to flesh out the whole picture. But our search is one of examining the details we have in the Scriptures in order to find all we can; that is, all Jesus Christ wanted us to have.

We will look at the Jerusalem church while it was under the control of the first Apostles. We will also examine other churches which the Apostles established. We shall thus see the growth of the forms and functions of the churches, while they followed the teachings and instructions of the Christian leaders who were personally taught by Jesus Himself. We shall not regard as pertinent those churches which came later than the apostolic period or which were established by anyone but the Twelve, those founded by St. Paul being the exception.

The final pattern for churches was put into practice by the Apostles, not within a year or two after the resurrection, but rather during the time of their far-flung planting of the Christian seed during their lifetimes. In that period, the nature of the church was enlarged and was adapted to various existential situations. There were great differences among the first-century churches, including those between Jewish and Gentile churches. Were these differences in the concept of the very nature of the churches or in unimportant policies? The answers may lie in how a person interprets the total New Testament, or perhaps no single pattern can be found. Certainly differences between churches in the apostolic age existed.

The great problem of so-called church history is that much of it was written long after the apostolic era, and practices which had crept into the churches in, say, the third or fourth centuries were read back into the descriptions of the New Testament era churches. Much of the ceremonialism practiced by the fourth century Christians was, perhaps, assumed to have been present in the New Testament era, but was actually unknown to the first-century congregations. (The *Didache*, an early non-canonical work, bears evidences of some very early ceremonial departures from the teaching of the New Testament, although

21

churches then generally agreed with it. This relatively "pure" reflection of first-century churches stands in contrast to later changes which came swiftly after the Apostles were gone.)

Church authority changed in concept rather early. St. Paul claimed apostolic authority, yet he denied having the right to dominate other Christians (see 2 Corinthians 1:24). Yet before long authoritarianism crept into the churches. The disavowal of such authority by St. Paul himself is fatal to the claim of an early universal hierarchy, as is also his description of his stinging public rebuke of St. Peter at Antioch (Galatians 2:11). Peter was surely not the *head* of any "universal church," which is itself a contradiction in terms.

But this is all old, well-plowed ground. What is important to this study is to see how as the Apostles spread the Gospel and established churches, there came to light universally valid principles of what the congregation generally ought to be.

THE SCOPE OF THIS STUDY

I have not tried to compile an encyclopedia of all the principles of the various early churches, but only those which were of major and lasting importance. We will follow, from the Book of Acts, the story of the development of the local church as an institution in the larger cities the Apostles visited. Additional light upon the local conditions in each of these important cities comes from the Epistles.

The thesis of this book involves the question, What did Jesus intend His churches to be?

Not one new or unique spiritual or doctrinal truth can be demonstrated to have been discovered since the apostolic age. Yet the forms and organizations of the churches have been changed ceaselessly. Is this the intended or even the permissive will of Christ? We are convinced it was not. At least not within the timeless principles of the primitive *ekklesia* wherever it was found.

It is the conviction of this writer that the vehicles of Christian truth—the apostolically founded congregations and their ministers—show us all that is needful today for faith, practice, form,

22

doctrine, and organization. These principles were fully revealed and divinely authenticated during the lifetimes of the Apostles and they have not changed, at least not with scriptural warrant.

Have the changes then which have occurred in the nature and mission of the churches since been good, bad, or mixed? Have these changes been based upon new insights into the once-and-for-all-delivered doctrines, or have they been imposed from prevailing cultures to the detriment of the church and its doctrines?

Have people since the apostolic age merely changed things in the church at will, rationalizing the changes by arguments not really germane to the intention of Christ?

Can we really understand the intent of the Holy Spirit for the church? Assuredly, we cannot conclude that the established churches have consistently and always understood that intent.

EXAMPLES OF THE DANGERS OF CHANGE IN THE CONCEPT OF THE EKKLESIA

The Spanish Inquisition, the rule of John Calvin over the secular city of Geneva, the behavior of churchmen in the period of the witch hangings of colonial America, the bloodshed of Henry VIII in England, the physical hounding of supposed heretics in various ages—all came from those who professed to hold fast to the authentic *doctrines* of Christianity. Whence then came these horrendous departures from the *spirit* of Christianity?

Obviously, they arose primarily from mistaken or perverted views of the church, held by those who otherwise stressed true Christian doctrine. Not one of those persons who so harmed Christianity officially denied the Faith (doctrine) of Christianity. What they did so despicably was to (supposedly) defend Christ *through the vehicle of the church!*

Could any of those excesses have occurred if their concept of the church had been that of the early Christians? We think not.

The union of church and state was and is a gross distortion of the New Testament understanding of the nature of the church.

Churches of the New Testament Era: Principles

The primitive church could and did exclude from fellowship the members who were unruly and heretical. But that was all. There was no inquisition, no trial by fire, no physical punishment. The early church was a redemptive local community of believers. When this concept gave way to a universal hierarchy, allied with or controlling the state, then the fundamental concept of the church itself obviously had been drastically altered. The true church never has had the right to the sword or to any other use of force.

Today that coercive tendency is rapidly disappearing. However, there remain many other significant additions to the concept of the church held by Christians in the apostolic age. Are they harmful or harmless?

It must be plain that the whole issue comes down to one question: Shall the principles of the early church, given by Christ and the Apostles, continue to be the ideal? Or are Christians to consider that while Christian *doctrine* was once and for all revealed, the *handling of the church* is entirely up to them, to retain or to change as they will?

How much change of the church is due to selfish ambition, to the almost irresistible impact of culture, the widespread indifference to (or ignorance of) the New Testament, or to the belief that the New Testament is not really sufficient? It is difficult to discern the motivations of those who have been agents of change. But questions should at least be considered thoughtfully.

THE TEST OF PRAGMATISM

Perhaps it also would be helpful to ask the practical question, What best preserves the truth of Christ—the early church and its principles faithfully followed, or an ever-changing church?

If it can be demonstrated pragmatically that following the pattern of the early churches works better to preserve and transmit the Faith, to bring people to Christ in an authentic way, then it is important to see accurately what the early churches were like.

That is the purpose of this study.

24

The Search for the Early Church

The church is weakened or polluted by individuals whose commitment, understanding, or surrender to the will of Christ is often imperfect, or who are impatient with the insights and enablement of the Holy Spirit.

Pure Christianity has a tremendous magnetism for those who are willing to see and to hear; great enough to inspire total commitment and surrender. But the centrifugal force working to take people from the center, Christ, is always present within man.

Christianity is more than mere doctrine and church organization. It is also a state of the heart. The teachings of Christ guide believers toward inner godliness and help the church to correctly understand itself and its mission.

Perhaps the pollution of the church begins when the main emphasis is placed upon the organization rather than upon the desired result, a changed state of heart and life in the believer and his participation in the congregation as a working member.

Christ is the example to individual believers. The Apostles were interpreters who were promised the unfolding revelation of the Holy Spirit. A composite study of New Testament churches and the answers to problems encountered by them can perhaps furnish the ideal prototype or "model" church. Are we not able therefore to summarize the solutions to the problems New Testament churches encountered, and emerge with a clearer view of what the church ought to be today?

Ekklesia ("those who are called out—called *together*") means not only that we are called apart from the world, but that we are called to come together as a body. The Holy Spirit draws people to fellowship through the magnet, Jesus Christ. It is important to make sure that the institution in which this magnetism is the main function and purpose does not hinder this work of the Spirit. The purpose of the church is to relate people to Christ and each other and to effectively to carry out His Kingdom's work.

The author on the Mount of Olives. A panoramic view of Jerusalem includes the Dome of the Rock, which stands upon a stone platform built by Herod the Great for his magnificent temple which Jesus called, "My Father's house."

Two
JERUSALEM

There were perhaps 120 people who formed the very first Christian church. We read that figure very early in the Book of Acts; it was the number of people gathered in the Upper Room awaiting the day of Pentecost (Acts 1:15). They were pastored by those who came to be called "Apostles," or "lightbearers." This group comprised the very first church, the *only* church that Jesus actually founded. Members of that church, sometimes led by Apostles and sometimes not, eventually went out from Jerusalem and founded churches all over the Roman world, as well as beyond the bounds of the Roman Empire.

THE APOSTLES AS CHURCH ORGANIZERS

My book *The Search for the Twelve Apostles* was based upon a study of what became of the first Apostles after the completion of the biblical record of their early ministries. Some of them traveled as far away as Persia; some went to India; some may actually have gone to Great Britain. Astonishingly, some went to the land which in those days was called Armenia. As a result of apostolic labors there, the very first country in the world to become officially Christian was Armenia. Today it is divided up between the Soviet Union, Turkey, and Iran. It is instructive to note that the land now called the Soviet Union had a witness to the Gospel of Jesus Christ by no less than five of the Apostles of Christ. One of them, Bartholomew, died there. What great adventures these early pioneers of the churches had! How far-reaching and long-lasting were the results of their church work!

Having traced their lives very carefully, from every scholarly source obtainable, this writer has concluded that without exception the one thing the Apostles did was to build churches—not buildings of course, but congregations. As far as the record reveals, in each city or populated area where some accepted the Gospel, the Apostles established a congregation.

THE IMPORTANCE OF THE CONGREGATION

We sometimes forget how very important the institution of the congregation (*ekklesia*) is in the sight of Jesus Christ. He did not entrust His Gospel to a government, perhaps because government's function is civil order, not religious faith. He did not call upon angels to proclaim the Gospel, probably because only those who have themselves been redeemed can proclaim the redeeming grace of God convincingly. He did not entrust this Gospel only to outstanding personalities, although the churches down through the centuries have had many. But instead He gave His Gospel to the *churches* to be preached until He would return. The church or congregation has always been the central instrument in the survival of the Gospel from generation to generation. This is a powerful lesson for Christians of the present time who so easily get distracted from the importance of the church.

Today's Christians have the churches in *their* hands. The question for them still is, as Jesus asked it, "When the Son of man returns, will He find the Faith on the earth?" That question was not answered by Him, because it was left to the decision of each generation of Christians to decide what that answer would be. One thing is sure—Christianity cannot long survive the death of the congregation in any place or land.

The Lord Jesus Christ, having looked at every human institution, means, and method by which the Gospel could be propagated when He went back to the Father to be our intercessor, chose above all things else to entrust it to the churches. For that reason the church is important. St. Paul said, "Christ also loved the church, and gave himself for it" (Ephesians 5:25).

If a person loves the Lord Jesus Christ, he will love what He loved. There is no greater cause in this world to challenge the very best that is in a Christian than to be a vital part of a church

28

of Jesus Christ, and to accept responsibility for its preservation and its work. Yet many modern-day Christians treat the Church with indifference, or take it for granted as they do such institutions as the post office.

THE CHURCH JESUS ESTABLISHED

As we have observed, the Jerusalem congregation was the only church which Jesus actually founded. To it He gave the task of fulfilling His promise that "greater works than I have done, ye shall do." That promise was fulfilled in Jerusalem and in many other churches, even to this day. This Jerusalem congregation had His teaching in its pristine freshness and the guidance of the Spirit-inspired Apostles.

Because of this, the Jerusalem church became a part of the divine pattern for other churches which later came into existence. Although there were things added to Christianity by the experience of other New Testament period churches, the Jerusalem church was the pioneer. In it were worked out the organizational patterns to be followed later by all true churches. We see this in its example at the Jerusalem Council (Acts 15) when the Apostles gave their verdict about the admission of believing Gentiles into the churches which were established by St. Paul and Barnabas.

The Jerusalem church survived for only a few years. It did not die because of neglect, disinterest, or lack of attendance but because of war. The Christians fled in A.D. 70 just before the Romans destroyed the city of Jerusalem from one end to the other.

People from many lands were in Jerusalem on the day of Pentecost when the first church began to grow in numbers. Three thousand were added to the membership of the Jerusalem church on that day alone. In their first flush of joy, they did not know that persecutions would scatter them to all parts of the Roman world. They did not know that the Jerusalem church, the parent church, would itself last only from approximately A.D. 33 to A.D. 70. It would have only thirty-seven years to do everything it was responsible to do.

29

Churches of the New Testament Era: Principles

Although the city of Jerusalem was destroyed, it has been re-built (and destroyed again) several times. But we know enough about it so that we can picture something of that city as the early Christians knew it. More importantly, we have the New Testament, especially the Book of Acts, to give us a fairly complete picture of the church there. What then characterized the early church in Jerusalem?

IT WAS AN EVANGELIZING, BAPTIZING CHURCH

On the day of Pentecost and on several important days thereafter, mention is made that the early church baptized people by the hundreds, and occasionally by the thousands. "Then they that gladly received his word were baptized: and the same day there were added unto them about three thousand souls" (Acts 2:41).

Jesus commanded His followers in the great commission, "Go ye therefore, and teach all nations, baptizing them in the name of the Father, and of the Son, and of the Holy Ghost: Teaching them to observe whatsoever things I have commanded you" (Matthew 28:19, 20).

IT REMAINED TRUE TO THE APOSTLES' DOCTRINE

Do we have a right to add to the Apostles' doctrine, that is, the body of the New Testament, if we proclaim ourselves to be Christians? If we add to their doctrine, the result is surely Christianity plus something else. Or if we take away from the Apostles' doctrine, we are preaching Christianity minus some things which are vital. Why be a minus or plus Christian—why not be simply a Christian? This is what C. S. Lewis implied by his memorable phrase, *"mere* Christianity."

The Apostles were inspired by the Holy Spirit, and Jesus promised that the Spirit would ". . . bring all things to your remembrance, whatsoever I have said unto you" (John 14:26). Then why assume we know more about how churches should be organized and run than the Apostles who received instruction from Jesus Himself? These early Christians ". . . continued steadfastly in the apostles' *doctrine* and fellowship, and in breaking of bread, and in prayers" (Acts 2:42).

IT WAS A CHURCH WHICH EMPHASIZED FELLOWSHIP

What is fellowship? It is enjoying the company of other people who have the same faith and who are related to you by the redeeming blood of Jesus Christ. They are, in fact, "blood relatives" who, like you, have trusted Christ as their Savior. It is not enough to be related to people as part of an *audience* in worship. Christians are brothers and sisters in Christ and are a *family* in fellowship. Or at least they should be. And no church today can be what Jesus wants His church to be unless it deliberately plans for and practices fellowship (Acts 2:42).

IT WAS A CHURCH WHICH ATE TOGETHER FREQUENTLY

"They continued . . . in breaking of bread" (Acts 2:42).

This is a biblical figure of speech, simply meaning to eat. I stress this because some churches are not like the early churches where members, according to the record, ate together frequently. It is still Christ's intention for the church today.

IT WAS A PRAYING CHURCH

Throughout the whole Book of Acts, it is recorded that the entire church met together for prayer. Prayer was continually made for the welfare and safety of the members. The church indeed was a praying institution.

Why do churches today have prayers in the services? It is because a true New Testament church is a church that knows how to lay hold upon God's promises, to present God with petitions and intercession.

This kind of earnest, seeking prayer is one of the things that we may have lost in the church. To be a New Testament church, we must pray together in faith.

IT WAS A SHARING, GIVING CHURCH

"And all that believed were together, and had all things common; And sold their possessions and goods, and parted them to all men, as every man had need" (Acts 2:44, 45).

In this period of time, it was very important that the first church be well started. To accomplish this, some people sold their property and gave the money in great amounts so that the church might gather momentum quickly. Such a means of giving and sharing meant that for a little while they chose to have many things in common. But this practice did not last. It was an emergency measure and not a permanent rule that would become a part of the churches forever.

We know this because in the record of all the rest of the New

Churches of the New Testament Era: Principles

Testament churches, while Christians often shared, they never again had their funds in common. Some people have mistakenly supposed that the Bible says the early Christians were communists. In no way was this true. While at first they had things in common for a few weeks or months, it was something they did because they were establishing Christianity. It wasn't a permanent feature or principle. Sharing, of course, has been practiced by Christians from that day to this.

Why was this early Christian practice of sharing not like communism or socialism? Because communism and socialism are political and coercive, and have the force of government behind them; whereas these early Christians shared with fellow believers because they wanted to. They were free not to do so or to do so, as Peter was very careful to tell Ananias and Sapphira in the Book of Acts: "While it [i.e., their property] remained, was it not thine own? and after it was sold, was it not in thine own power? why hast thou conceived this thing in thine heart? thou hast not lied unto men, but unto God" (Acts 5:4). Personal rights to property (i.e., what one owns or controls) are respected consistently throughout the entire Bible.

You can find many instances of "sharing," such as: "And all that believed were together, and had all things common" (Acts 2:44). "Neither was there any among them that lacked: for as many as were possessors of lands or houses sold them, and brought the prices of the things that were sold" (Acts 4:34). "And in those days, when the number of the disciples was multiplied, there arose a murmuring of the Grecians against the Hebrews, because their widows were neglected in the daily ministration" (Acts 6:1). "Only they would that we should remember the poor; the same which I also was forward to do" (Galatians 2:10). "Pure religion and undefiled before God and the Father is this, To visit the fatherless and widows in their affliction, and to keep himself unspotted from the world" (James 1:27).

Over and over again, this principle of Christians freely sharing with God's people is mentioned favorably.

IT WAS A CHURCH WITH A DAILY PROGRAM OF ACTIVITIES

There was a continuous program of witnessing and evangelism in the Jerusalem church. The members worshiped daily, conducting meetings in their houses as well as in the Temple. "And they, continuing daily with one accord in the temple, and breaking bread from house to house, did eat their meat with gladness and singleness of heart; praising God and having favor with all the people. And the Lord added to the church daily such as should be saved" (Acts 2:46, 47).

The Jerusalem church had a day by day program, not just on Sunday, not just on the Sabbath (Saturday). *Every day* people were won to Christ; *every day* they had house meetings and prayer meetings. *Every day* they were in the Temple.

IT WAS A CHURCH WHICH FEATURED DIVINE HEALING

"And his name, through faith in his name, hath made this man strong, whom ye see and know: yea, the faith which is by him hath given him this perfect soundness in the presence of you all" (Acts 3:16).

St. Peter was talking about a lame man who was healed at the Golden Gate. The Jerusalem church practiced divine healing. We find this throughout the New Testament.

"For the man was above forty years old, on whom this miracle of healing was showed" (Acts 4:22). "There came also a multitude out of the cities round about unto Jerusalem, bringing sick folks, and them which were vexed with unclean spirits: and they were healed every one" (Acts 5:16). "Is any sick among you? let him call for the elders of the church; and let them pray over him, anointing him with oil in the name of the Lord" (James 5:14).

Other examples may be found in many, many other places in the New Testament.

IT WAS A CHURCH WHICH WITNESSED BOLDLY

"And when they had prayed, the place was shaken where they were assembled together; and they were all filled with the Holy Spirit, and they spake the word of God with boldness" (Acts 4:31).

Are you bold in your proclamation of the Scriptures and in your testimony of your faith and experience in Christ? Or are you ashamed of the Gospel? Why is it we are ashamed of Christ when Christ is the power of God unto salvation? Whoever was ashamed of power since the world began? And that is what salvation is—God's power in your life.

Churches of the New Testament Era: Principles

"For whosoever shall be ashamed of me and of my words, of him shall the Son of man be ashamed, when he shall come in his own glory, and in his Father's, and of the holy angels" (Luke 9:26).

Are you ashamed to say, "Yes, I will publicly accept Jesus as my Savior and my Lord"?

In that early church, one of its characteristics was that "they spake the word of God with boldness," and on many occasions they had to go to jail for doing so. James had his head cut off, and Stephen was stoned to death. Yet believers stood up and proclaimed the Word of God boldly.

IT WAS A TEACHING CHURCH

"Then came one and told them, saying, Behold, the men whom ye put in prison are standing in the temple, and teaching the people" (Acts 5:25).

They were teaching people in the Temple. There is our authorization for Sunday school and other teaching programs.

IT WAS A VOTING CHURCH

A social problem arose quickly within the Jerusalem church. It involved caring for two kinds of widows—the widows who were Greeks, and those who were Jewish. At first, Jewish Christians and Greek Christians didn't get along too well with one another. The Jews were in the majority and apparently took advantage of the minority of Greek widows.

The Apostles stood up before the congregation and said, "This is our suggestion." Notice how they approached the people—with a suggestion, not a command. "Wherefore, brethren, look ye out among you seven men of honest report, full of the Holy Ghost and wisdom, whom we may appoint over this business" (Acts 6:3).

These men had to be known to be fair and honest, because there was a question of who was receiving the most food. They were also to be men who were "full of the Holy Spirit and wisdom."

God's work, then and now, requires God's power and wisdom if a mighty work is to be done.

These men, chosen by the people, were the first deacons. Their job was to take care of the material well-being of the church. The deacons were established as an order within the early church by the direction of the Holy Spirit under the leadership of the Apostles, but approved and selected by the vote of the congregation. The Apostles explained the need and their own authority in these words, "whom we may appoint over this business. But we will give ourselves continually to prayer, and to the ministry of the word."

Note the next few verses, because they are the foundation of the principle of democracy in the early church:

"And they chose Stephen, a man full of faith and of the Holy Ghost, and Philip, and Prochorus, and Nicanor, and Timon, and Parmenas, and Nicolas a proselyte of Antioch; whom they set before the apostles: and when they had prayed, they laid their hands on them. And the word of God increased; and the number of the disciples multiplied in Jerusalem greatly; and a great company of the priests were obedient to the faith" (Acts 6:5-7).

The deacons as a body of men were selected by the church and ordained by the Apostles, who were elders. But note this—when it says they "chose" Stephen and the others, in the original Greek the phrase is, "by vote of the hand." They chose by *voting*. Where did we derive the principle of congregational voting? From the early church in Jerusalem. There are other examples of this, such as: "Then pleased it the apostles and elders, *with the whole church*, to send chosen men of their own company to Antioch with Paul and Barnabas; namely, Judas surnamed Barsabas, and Silas, chief men among the brethren" (Acts 15:22).

The word "deacon" means servant, and the word "minister" also means servant. These are two words which in the original language meant the same thing. The deacons and ministers were the servants of the church. The congregation, however, was the final authority on matters concerning the management of the church.

IT WAS A CHURCH SPIRITUALLY LED BY ELDERS

The Jerusalem church had a multiplicity of "elders" or spiritual leaders. In the church in Jerusalem, this refers primarily to the Apostles. St. Peter wrote, "I who am also an elder" (1 Peter 5:1). An elder is someone who has been set aside by a special ordination to lead the people of God, by teaching, preaching, guidance, and leadership. "Elder" literally means "an older person." The New Testament gives a full description of what the elders are to be. The word primarily means a mature leader of the congregation to whom the congregation gives the right to teach, preach, and manage nonfinancial church affairs (the finances are the responsibility of the deacons).

But note: the early church had a system of multiple elders. It never had just one elder. There is another name for an elder who is the chairman of the elders, and that is the word "bishop." The bishop was the senior minister of the elders in the New Testament era. A local church had one bishop and several elders. The words "elder," "minister," "pastor," and "bishop" all denote more or less the same office, with only shades or variations of meaning and responsibility. Many denominations have changed the historic meaning of these offices, but what we have observed here is what the New Testament teaches about these roles in the church. Upon these apostolic principles, directed into new situations by the Apostles themselves, Christianity spread in the first century.

The Jerusalem church became the great foundation pattern for all churches.

The Jerusalem church shows us the divine authorization for what we should do.

It is most important that we understand what *this* New Testament church was like, because the foundation of our churches today, our roots and our practices originate with, and therefore should go back to, the principles of the Jerusalem church.

SUMMARY

We have set forth the twelve great principles of the New Testament church which were found in the Jerusalem church and which, by the grace of God, we should have in our churches.

In today's churches, a problem arises when the clergy are placed in full control of everything. The Holy Spirit then may not have room in which to work through whomsoever He wishes. When a church writes a rulebook, there is the possibility that the church may become so hidebound that even God

36

Jerusalem

Himself can't come in and do His will, because there seems always to be a rule to keep Him out. Churches should ideally believe that power belongs to the members of the church, who in turn believe that the New Testament is all-sufficient for faith, order, program, policy, and all other things, including doctrine, which comes from Christ and the Spirit-inspired Apostles.

Some rules for the church are helpful and needed, so that all things may be "done decently and in order"; but the rules should also be flexible enough to leave room for the leadership of the Holy Spirit.

The rest of the churches of the New Testament period were organized on the foundation and after the pattern of the Jerusalem church. Denominations did not yet exist.

The Scroll of the Pentateuch owned by the dwindling cult of the Samaritans who live in Nablus, near Mount Ebal and Mount Gerizim.

Three
SAMARIA

It was a momentous day in Christian history. Jesus gathered His disciples together for the last time and took them up to the Mount of Olives. His final words were these: "Be witnesses unto Me in Jerusalem, in Judea, and *Samaria.*" How that very familiar biblical name drops smoothly into place; few pay any real attention to it.

Do you understand the significance of what He said? Jesus was referring to the natural geographical order one encountered on the great highway to Galilee. "Start where you are in Jerusalem. Then go into Judea. Then evangelize the next big area and city to the north." Jesus' very commandment came to be fulfilled as if it were a prophecy.

The church in Jerusalem was founded on the day of Pentecost. At that feast, there were visitors in Jerusalem from all over the Roman world. Those people, mostly Jews, heard the Christian message, returned to their faraway homes, and (if they now knew Christ) began to witness. The very first district on their journey, if they went north, was Samaria. Undoubtedly some who were in Jerusalem for Pentecost were from that area and were among the first believers.

What was the special significance of Samaria? Everybody recognizes it, obviously, as the home of the Samaritans. "The good Samaritan" came from there. The story of the beginnings of Christianity there are told us in detail in Acts 8. This was about the time when Saul of Tarsus was persecuting the church in Jerusalem. He had not yet been converted to Christ and had not yet come to be called Paul. The narrative in Acts observes, "... and they were all scattered abroad throughout the regions of Judea and Samaria, except the apostles" (Acts 8:1).

The Jerusalem church had probably continued to grow for

four or five years, until one day persecution arose; then many of the Christians were forced to flee Jerusalem. The Apostles remained quietly behind. Who were those Christians who fled? They were what some people today would call "laymen" because they were not Apostles or "full-time" ministers.

In our own time, we can still see examples of persecuted Christians establishing new churches in lands to which they flee. For example, at the outset of World War II there were few churches in Hawaii. When the Japanese took mainland China, and then moved on to conquer Singapore, the Philippines, and other parts of Asia, many American missionaries were forced to evacuate. While waiting for the war to end, many lived for a time in Hawaii. They found that there were not nearly enough churches on the islands, so missionaries from China and the Philippines and other places started churches in Hawaii. Like the early Christians when they were scattered abroad, these missionaries went everywhere preaching the Word.

If you were to find yourself in a foreign city where there was no witness for Christ, would you have a prayer meeting in your home with some other person who was interested, and then find still others, and finally start a church? If you would not, you are not like the early Christians, because that is what they did.

Let us read the interesting story about what happened to the first church to be formed after the Jerusalem church: "Then Philip went down to the city of Samaria, and preached Christ unto them. And the people with one accord gave heed unto those things which Philip spake, hearing and seeing the miracles which he did" (8:4, 5).

What are the universal principles for all churches which can be learned from this church?

FIVE GREAT PRINCIPLES REVEALED IN THE CHURCH AT SAMARIA

First: *Many of the churches of the early days, particularly this church, were started by laymen with the guidance of the Apostles.* The Apostles were indeed helpful in terms of giving direction, doctrine, good order, and organization to the church; but the church at Samaria was begun by Christian laymen who were not apostles or trained pastors. This principle, stated briefly, was that Christianity does not entirely depend upon the clergy.

Second: We are told exactly what Philip preached— *"preaching the things concerning the kingdom of God, and the name of Jesus Christ"* (vs. 12). That is still the message today: make God the King of your life, for someday God is going to be King over all the earth. Satan is a usurper, and the earth is an area of the universe which he has taken by "squatter's rights," revolution, and rebellion. But actually the world belongs to God. Someday He's going to bind Satan and make the earth the center of His millennial Kingdom.

Paul wrote to Timothy, "Preach the Word." This is also what Philip preached—the "Word" about Christ and His Kingdom. The need for this has not changed.

Third: We are in the very dawn of Christian history when we observe events in this old city of Samaria. In the Jewish synagogues and in the Samaritan synagogue, women attended but were not permitted to take an active part in the worship service. But when the Gospel came to Samaria, "both men *and women*" were baptized (vs. 12). That means they were baptized into the church, because baptism was the only way in those days by which people were received into church membership. As they were baptized, it signified that they were joining the church. This is where Christianity broke with Judaism. *Both men and women were taken into full fellowship and membership in the early church*; women were no longer restricted because of gender.

Paul could write in his full maturity of experience, much later, that in Christ "there is neither Jew nor Greek, there is neither bond nor free, there is neither male nor female; for ye are all one in Christ Jesus" (Galatians 3:28).

If Christians in any century have practiced discrimination against women, it is because they have been less Christian than the early churches. Men and women had certain distinctive jobs that each did in the early church, but there was no discrimination evident in the biblical record.

Some ancient Jews used to say, "I thank God every day that

Churches of the New Testament Era: Principles

I was not born a dog, a Gentile, or a woman." Christians did not feel this way.

In the very beginning of Christianity, in the very first churches, the concept was taught of both the "new man" and "new woman" in Christ. Old shackles and old concepts were laid aside.

Do you see why it is important that we understand the early churches? How easily down through the ages of Christian history some believers have lost sight of those churches' characteristics. So many of the abuses, so many of the social evils in which Christians have participated would never have arisen if these Christians had only followed the early churches. For example, we would not have the unnecessary division between "clergy" and "laity" which is one of the weaknesses of Christianity today.

Fourth: The Holy Spirit came upon the believers (vs. 17). Who were "the believers"? This wasn't Jerusalem, where pure Jews lived. This was Samaria, the home of Samaritans, half-Jews. At that time, the Jews by and large did not hold the Samaritans in high esteem. That attitude persists to this day. The Samaritans were partly Israelite because they came from all the tribes, and partly Canaanite; hence, they were a racial mixture. The Jews considered them mongrels.

Furthermore, Samaritans did not have as much of the truth as the Jews possessed, because they accepted only the first five books of the Bible, the laws of Moses. They had none of the prophets, nor the Psalms or other books of the Old Testament. And they were fanatic about worshiping only on two mountains, Mount Gerizim and its opposite, Mount Ebal. They were spiritually both uninstructed and provincial. As the Gospel spread and the first church outside of Jerusalem was established among people who were called "mongrels," probably one of the first members of that church was the "woman at the well." Jesus had said to her that she was little better than a harlot. But she was undoubtedly accepted into full fellowship by the church because of her repentance. You can see how the Gospel broke down racial, social, and sexual barriers.

Man-made walls of division, labeling some people "unclean," fall down when men and women come to faith in Christ; those

Samaria

same people are called precious by the Lord Jesus Christ. Does that say anything to you about the principles of the early church? It should. *The Samaritan church was established among people who were virtual religious and social outcasts*, although they were not Gentiles in the strictest sense.

Fifth: The gifts of God would always be freely given and would never be for sale. In Samaria, Simon the sorcerer, a nominal convert, tried to buy the power of the Holy Spirit. Peter sternly said, " . . . for thy heart is not right in the sight of God. . . . For I perceive that thou art in the gall of bitterness, and in the bond of iniquity" (vv. 21, 23).

To receive the gifts of God, the only requirement is that one's heart be right in God's sight. And that principle is still true today in our churches.

For the teenager who is beginning to face the battles and temptations of life, we ask, "Is your heart right with God?" That is all that is necessary to make you eligible for God's power to come into your life. We ask the older Christian who has been walking with God for a long time, "Have you grown stale? Are you as zealous as you were? Have you lost your first love? *Is your heart right with God?*" That is the universal principle upon which the true church should operate today, because it was the principle on which the early churches operated.

Are these principles at work in your life, in your heart, and in your church?

Have you raised your eyes to look on the harvest field and to see that the harvest is plenteous? Are you disturbed by that? Have you asked the Lord of the harvest to send forth laborers into His harvest? Have you said, "Here am I, Lord; send me"?

The ancient Roman bridge at Antioch.

Four
ANTIOCH

The mysterious, first-century city of Antioch, located in Turkey near the Syrian border, was on one of the greatest Roman highways, some portions of which still remain to this day.

It is said that it was the only city in the Roman Empire which had streetlights. At one time, Antioch was the third largest city in the Empire, after Alexandria and Rome itself. From Antioch westward, through Tarsus (the birthplace of St. Paul) and through the Cilician Gates, over a narrow road providing the only way into the interior of Turkey, the Roman highway led all the way to Italy. Antioch stood as the eastern terminus of that road. Beyond it to the east lay Syria, Babylonia, and Persia. By land, one could travel from Rome to Antioch and then south all the way to Jerusalem and even Arabia; but in all cases, whether coming or going, the great city one must sooner or later pass through was Antioch.

Its inhabitants were a mixture of all the peoples of the Empire —Greeks, Persians, Romans, Jews, Syrians, and even Russians, or Scythians as they were called then.

Jerusalem, Athens, and Rome were important cities then and now. Antioch, however, is now only a country town, its highway seldom traveled, and most of its Roman-Greek heritage visible only when the archaeologists have done their work. In the ancient city, as now, a great river coursed straight through the main part of the town. Not far away were the infamous Groves of Daphne, where idolatry and temple prostitution were rampant. Today those groves still exist, as the largest picnic grounds and park in eastern Turkey, although the temples and idols were destroyed long ago.

Antioch is in the best watered and most fertile part of Turkey,

45

because of the Orontes River and the thousand springs and waterfalls of Daphne.

Early in Christian history, some unknown Christians, driven from Jerusalem by persecution, came to Antioch and witnessed for Christ in the Jewish synagogue. Many Jews there became believers. Before long, many Gentiles who were converts to Judaism also came to Christ. Then their relatives and friends, pagans, also became Christians in great numbers.

Since this was the first city where this type of mixed congregation evolved, the Apostles and other elders in Jerusalem heard of it and dispatched Barnabas to minister there. Barnabas, surprised at the size of the church, sent for Saul, who was dwelling at Tarsus nearby. Saul was not welcome in Jerusalem, being looked upon as a traitor by the Sanhedrin and with suspicion by the Jerusalem Christians. But now Saul's eight years of exile and contemplation were to end. Before long he was to become one of the chief figures in early Christianity. It was in Antioch where he was first warmly welcomed, where he preached and taught, and from which each of his three famed missionary journeys began (and where they ended).

Paul must have loved the church at Antioch. It was his base of operations, the place of his ordination to become the greatest of all missionaries. There he often renewed himself in Christian fellowship, and received financial and prayer support; no matter how far he traveled, he found himself sooner or later back in Antioch.

It seems strange but (perhaps due to the remoteness of Antioch in today's world) many Christians are not aware of the Antioch church's importance to the Christian cause during the first century, especially in those decisive fourth and fifth decades. Next to Jerusalem itself, it was the most important city for Christianity in the entire first century, as a careful reading of the Book of Acts will reveal. Why?

1. *Antioch was the city where Christians were first called by that name* (Acts 11:26). Up until this time whenever people were referred to as followers of Jesus, they were called "Nazarenes," or "followers of the Way."

In the Book of Acts, the phrase "the Way" is the earliest name for Christianity. But because "the Way" could mean almost anything, in Antioch they came to be called after the name of "Christ," meaning the "Messiah." "Christians" are those who accept Jesus as the Messiah. Notably, they received the name "Christian" in Antioch, not in Jerusalem.

2. *It was the first church where believing Jews and converts from Gentile paganism came together and formed one congregation.* Most American Christians have descended from Europeans; our ancestors have not worshiped idols for a long time. But some American Christians are from Africa, some from Asia; and their ancestors perhaps worshiped idols more recently. But now in Christ we are all one family; we have one Father—God Who became our spiritual Father when we put our trust in Jesus. We became brothers and sisters—never mind who our parents are, or who our ancestors may have been. When we put our faith in Jesus Christ, we become vitally related to each other; that relationship was on display in Antioch. What a glorious principle emerged in that great church for all true churches to come!

3. *It was the first church outside Palestine to engage in Christian charity.* In the early life of the Jerusalem church, the widows were cared for and given food. But among all the churches founded by the early Christians, Antioch was the first to send help to the suffering saints in Jerusalem, and hence to practice Christian charity to someone outside their own circle.

This church at Antioch saw that Christian charity—care for the physical needs of Christians suffering in Jerusalem—was not only a duty, but a blessed privilege for all those in Christ. Churches have been practicing it ever since.

4. *The church at Antioch was the first missionary church.* A chapter in my book *The Search for the Twelve Apostles* discusses the question of just when the Apostles left Jerusalem for the far-flung mission fields of the world. Why did the Apostles stay in Jerusalem so long when Jesus had told them, "Go out to all the world and preach the Gospel"? God had to send some persecution along before they were willing to obey. When they finally went out, they witnessed only to Jews at first. So the Holy Spirit had to push them, through circumstances, into winning Gentiles to Christ.

Jesus had said, "Go ye therefore, and teach all nations, baptizing them in the name of the Father, and of the Son, and of the Holy Ghost: Teaching them to observe all things whatsoever I have commanded you; and, lo, I am with you alway, even unto the end of the world. Amen" (Matthew 28:19, 20).

The promise that Jesus Christ would be with His disciples *was made to those who would go*, disciple, baptize, and win *all* people. "Red and yellow, black and white," as we sang in Sunday school, "all are precious in His sight." And this ministry of foreign missions began in Antioch.

The greatest missionary and the greatest evangelist who ever lived was St. Paul. Antioch was his home base. This is where the Holy Spirit said, "Now separate Paul and Barnabas unto Me and send them." The church people obediently dug into their pockets, came up with the money, and sent them. Paul started churches like a string of pearls all over the route of the circle which he traveled on his first journey. But the pearls led back home and clasped together at Antioch.

Then the second missionary journey led Paul and Silas out to a larger area, and the third to an even larger one; but always they came back home to Antioch. There Paul's spirit was refreshed; there he was given additional financial help; there he was given the backing, the support, and the prayers he needed as a missionary. In effect, the Holy Spirit directed that Antioch was to be the starting place for it all.

5. *It was a giving church*. I was disappointed when I first went to Antioch. Today it is a Moslem city, and there is not a church in the town. How sad it seems! But the reason lies in history—in the wars of the Middle Ages, and in the Moslem conquest. If we could go back in imagination to visit the ancient church after it had been well established, we would again cross the old Roman bridge, and perhaps visit some of the Groves of Daphne where paganism ruled. Then perhaps we might go to a large house and gather with the ancient Christians. What would we be impressed with or notice? In a very unique sense, setting a pattern for all Christians to come, we would find it was a giving church! And we would feel right at home, for our churches today are also giving institutions.

We don't know how Barnabas raised the first offering for evangelism or how Paul secured his missionary funds, but we

Antioch

do know they received generous contributions from the Christians in that church in Antioch.

The church also gave the Gospel to the Gentiles. Their leaders didn't say, "Gentiles, you're not Jews and therefore, even if you accept Christ, you can't come into the church." Instead they said, "The door is wide open; come in!" And it was the first church in the world said to have done that, except Jerusalem.

The church also gave to foreign missions. Without the help of those members, Paul and Barnabas could not have undertaken that first missionary journey, or the other missionary journeys which followed. Paul earned his living when he stayed a long time in any one town, but the expenses of his initial traveling and moving about were covered by the Antioch church.

As a contemporary Christian, you stand squarely in the tradition of this great church at Antioch. When you do, God is still happy to call you "Christian," as He was happy to claim those ancient believers as His own.

The main street of the most ancient section of Joppa.

Five
JOPPA AND CAESAREA

The Book of Acts was laid out by its author to emphasize certain happenings in the expansion of early Christianity; namely, to show how it began within Judaism and then began to be proclaimed to all mankind.

The first part of Acts deals with Jerusalem, where the chief spokesman of the local church was St. Peter. The second division focuses on the church at Antioch; from that base of operations the central figure was St. Paul. There are many overlappings. St. Paul and St. Peter met in Jerusalem at least three times and at Antioch once. Their paths also crossed in terms of the areas of their ministries, notably at Corinth and Rome.

St. Paul preached to many Jews, everywhere he went, but was primarily known as the Apostle to the Gentiles. St. Peter won many Jews and also many Gentiles, though at first he was primarily an Apostle to the Jews. In fact, they were both present when a temporary agreement was reached at an important conference of the Apostles in Jerusalem, as St. Paul writes in Galatians 2:9: "And when James, Cephas [i.e., Peter], and John, who seemed to be pillars, perceived the grace that was given unto me, they gave to me and Barnabas the right hands of fellowship; that we should go unto the heathen, and they unto the circumcision."

We must not conclude that St. Peter never went to the Gentiles. As St. Paul first extended the Gospel to the Gentiles beginning at Antioch, so Peter, probably much earlier, had likewise preached the Gospel to Gentiles in Palestine. The story is found in Acts 9, 10, describing St. Peter on an evangelistic tour of the seacoast area of Lydda (near Lod today), Joppa (near Tel Aviv today), and Caesarea (the main Roman port then, a ruin today).

There were a number of churches in that area before St. Peter

51

Churches of the New Testament Era: Principles

visited. During his ministry at Caesarea, at least one predominantly Gentile congregation was formed. There were also Jews in it, as was the case in Antioch far to the north. (Athens also was the site of a Gentile church, even though it was extremely small during St. Paul's brief ministry there.)

In any case, both for St. Paul and for St. Peter, the guidance of the Holy Spirit was most explicit: the Gentiles were to be included in the membership of the early churches.

What principles came to light during St. Peter's ministry in the coastal area of the Holy Land? The Book of Acts mentions several.

1. In Lydda the church is described as *composed of "saints"* (Acts 9:32). This phrase is used many times in the New Testament and in those days meant "holy ones"; that is, those who were set aside for God by their personal surrender to Christ. Thus the authority for true Christians, while yet alive, to be called saints. The later practice of canonization was unknown in the New Testament.

2. St. Peter healed a Greek (vs. 33), possibly already a member of the congregation, thus further demonstrating the *divine acceptance of the Greek believers*.

3. At Joppa, St. Peter *restored to life* a prominent Jewish woman, a member of the congregation who had died (vv. 36-41). She was a charitable worker whose Christianity was expressed in a river of good deeds. Thus, her resurrection illustrated God's blessing upon those whose personal *agape* sustains the Christian poor, an important principle in the early churches and in the church today.

4. Peter was specifically instructed through a vision from God and the salvation of Cornelius, a Roman centurion at Caesarea, that *God had accepted the piety and sincerity of Gentiles* who were readily receptive to the Christian message when it was explained to them (Chapter 10). It is important to note that piety was accepted, not as the way of salvation—which came by faith in Christ alone—but as the proper attitude which led the pious *to Christ*. (See Acts 10:31.) The saving message of St. Peter was clear: "preaching peace by Jesus Christ: (he is Lord of all)" (vs. 36).

5. Cornelius mistakenly tried to worship Peter when they

52

Joppa and Caesarea

met. Peter refused it, saying, " . . . I myself also am a man" (vs. 26).

If the living Apostle would not accept worship, then how can man worship those dead Christians who are "canonized" by a religious organization? The worship of either living or dead saints was *not* a part of the early churches.

6. *The Holy Spirit came upon Jews and Gentiles alike*, thus establishing equality of both before the Lord and in the church: "While Peter yet spake these words, the Holy Ghost fell on all them which heard the word" (vs. 44).

7. The early church in Caesarea, in the home of Cornelius, probably *the first mainly Gentile church*, was composed of Cornelius' family, friends, and employees. "And the morrow after they entered into Caesarea. And Cornelius waited for them, and had called together his kinsmen and near friends" (vs. 24).

The traditional prison at Philippi where Paul and Silas preached Christ to their jailer.

Six
PHILIPPI

The first "house church" of Europe (see Acts 16:6-40) gathered in the home of Lydia, a woman of Philippi in Macedonia, Greece.

"And when she was baptized, and her household, she besought us, saying, If ye have judged me to be faithful to the Lord, come into my house, and abide there. And she constrained us" (vs. 15).

Lydia was already a worshiper of God, perhaps with other proselytes as well as with the few Jews who lived there. With them, she was worshiping God by the riverside on the Sabbath day, a practice followed only by Jews and those who prayed to God with them. There was no synagogue in Philippi, or the group would not have resorted to the river site in what was probably a public park.

Three remarkable conversions are described in Acts 16, each very different from the others, and doubtless were recorded in the account for very good reasons.

Lydia and her household. "And they went out of the prison, and entered into the house of Lydia: and when they had seen the brethren, they comforted them, and departed" (vs. 40). Judging from the fact that Paul was able to baptize Lydia's "household" who are later spoken of as "brethren," there must have been a number of men and, of course, women. No infants are mentioned or implied in the record.

The demon-possessed young woman. Her peculiar demonic possession seemed to give her the gift of divination or fortune-telling. When the evil spirit was exorcised, the woman apparently lost the ability to foretell the future. No record is given of her baptism and, in fact, nothing more is recorded about her in the Bible. However, it is most unlikely that she would not have

Churches of the New Testament Era: Principles

joined the church, considering her anguished profession of faith, "The same followed Paul and us, and cried, saying, These men are the servants of the most high God, which show unto us the way of salvation" (vs. 17).

The jailer. Jailers in that day were rough and brutal men. The profession demanded that the jailer guard his prisoners perfectly; if any escaped, he would have to forfeit his own life.

"And the keeper of the prison awaking out of his sleep, and seeing the prison doors open, he drew out his sword, and would have killed himself, supposing that the prisoners had been fled" (vs. 27). "And they spake unto him the word of the Lord, and to all that were in his house" (vs. 32).

Since the record tells us that Paul and Silas spoke the Word, the hearers were evidently old enough to believe. Then the jailer and his family were baptized immediately. "And he took them the same hour of the night, and washed their stripes; and was baptized, he and all his, straightway" (vs. 33).

The universal principles found in the church at Philippi are these:

1. *Immediate baptism.* In each conversion there was first a witness or instruction by Paul and Silas. Baptism took place immediately—there was no prolonged period of probation deemed necessary. Baptism was not practiced apart from instruction and a response of faith.

2. *Crossing all social lines.* This was obvious in this church. A woman originally from Thyatira (Lydia, a woman who sold purple dye, a product of Thyatira then and now) was the head of a large household and owned a spacious house where the church could meet. The jailer also had a house, but the "household" was evidently small since all were baptized at night—perhaps in the rushing stream, but also possibly in a water trough nearby. It is unlikely that the religious Lydia and the jailer had very much in common socially.

Neither, of course, would have previously known the unfortunate fortune-telling maid. This mixture of social groups, plus those who were the household relatives and servants, made up the church. Perhaps even slaves were involved. This remarkable church, which was to know St. Luke, Timothy, Titus, and other apostolic leaders, was the church St. Paul apparently loved best of all. "Even as it is meet for me to think this of you all, because I have you in my heart; inasmuch as both in my bonds, and in the defense and confirmation of the gospel, ye all are partakers of my grace" (Philippians 1:7).

This love is revealed in his letter to them, and in his loving reference to them in the letter to the Corinthians. The social mixture of people unlike each other was frequently on Paul's mind.

"Only let your conversation be as it becometh the gospel of Christ: that whether I come and see you, or else be absent, I may hear of your affairs, that ye stand fast in one spirit, with one mind striving together for the faith of the gospel" (Philippians 1:27).

"Moreover, brethren, we do you to wit of the grace of God bestowed on the churches of Macedonia; How that in a great trial of affliction, the abundance of their joy and their deep poverty abounded unto the riches of their liberality. For to their power, I bear record, yea, and beyond their power they were willing of themselves; Praying us with much entreaty that we would receive the gift, and take upon us the fellowship of the ministering to the saints. And this they did, not as we hoped, but first gave their own selves to the Lord, and unto us by the will of God" (2 Corinthians 8:1-5).

"Let nothing be done through strife or vainglory; but in lowliness of mind let each esteem other better than themselves. Look not every man on his own things, but every man also on the things of others" (Philippians 2:3, 4).

3. *Continued stewardship*. The church at Philippi supplied the Apostle Paul willingly, generously, and continuously.

"And when I was present with you, and wanted, I was chargeable to no man: for that which was lacking to me the brethren which came from Macedonia supplied: and in all things I have kept myself from being burdensome unto you, and so will I keep myself" (2 Corinthians 11:9).

"Even as it is meet for me to think this of you all, because I have you in my heart; inasmuch as both in my bonds, and in the defense and confirmation of the gospel, ye all are partakers of my grace" (Philippians 1:7).

"Now ye Philippians know also, that in the beginning of the

Churches of the New Testament Era: Principles

gospel, when I departed from Macedonia, no church communicated with me as concerning giving and receiving, but ye only" (Philippians 4:15).

4. *The "indigenous" church*. The church at Philippi was evidently self-perpetuating and grew under its own leadership. St. Paul told the Corinthians that he would visit Macedonia, and very likely wrote 1 Corinthians while there. Scholars believe from the "we" passages in Acts 16, 17 that St. Luke stayed on in Philippi after Paul and Silas departed for Berea. By the time St. Paul wrote his Epistle to the Philippians, there is every indication that the Philippian church was fully mature with its own inner momentum, assisted by members of Paul's team only from time to time. Why do we say this?

It had its own bishops and deacons. "Paul and Timotheus, the servants of Jesus Christ, to all the saints in Christ Jesus which are at Philippi, with the bishops and deacons" (Philippians 1:1).

Well-known Christians arose from their midst, including Epaphroditus. "Yet I supposed it necessary to send to you Epaphroditus, my brother, and companion in labor, and fellow soldier, but your messenger, and he that ministered to my wants" (Philippians 2:25). This man of God later went to Rome as the messenger of the Philippian church.

Paul also mentions Clement (4:3), who became the leading pastor in Rome well after the deaths of St. Peter and St. Paul, and who probably wrote the first-century Epistle of Clement which still survives.

Two women of prominence, who seemed to be at odds with each other, are also named. "I beseech Euodias, and beseech Syntyche, that they be of the same mind in the Lord" (Philippians 4:2). Individualism was present, as befits a mature church, provided Christian principles prevail.

The church at Philippi was a strong anchor of the Christian movement. Philippi was a Roman colony (Acts 16:12) and was very prominent in both Greece and in the Roman Empire. Here a great battle between factions of the Roman civil war had settled the destiny of the Empire long before St. Paul came to evangelize the city. The principle of indigenous autonomy with maturity, stewardship, and self-perpetuation in that strategic and strong church shows the paths to a strong church today.

Philippi

Beginning as a Jewish congregation and rapidly growing to include Greeks, Philippi was also a church with a definite Roman membership (though a minority) and with eventual strong ties to Rome by means of Paul, Luke, Epaphroditus, and Clement. It had an influence far beyond its environs. This too is a frequent if not universal mark of all the important churches of the apostolic age.

The main street of Thessalonika, showing the ruins of an ancient triumphal arch.

Seven
THESSALONIKA

Though St. Paul had ministered to the church in Thessalonika for only about one month before opposition made it necessary for him to flee to Berea, he left behind a solidly organized church in this chief port city in northern Greece. Then, as now, the city was the second largest in Greece after Athens. Like Athens, it maintained communication with all major countries of the eastern Mediterranean, including Israel.

Consequently, there were large numbers of Jewish traders, settlers, and immigrants who lived in Thessalonika. Further, there was a Jewish synagogue there that was evidently in communication with Jewish authorities in Jerusalem. The enmity expressed toward St. Paul probably came from Jews who received word from Jerusalem that the Christian movement was considered as opposed to Judaism.

Thessalonika was undoubtedly a city of wealth, and the Jews shared in that. To this day, there are large numbers of Jews in the city and consequently several synagogues even now.

Paul came to Thessalonika from Philippi, in line with his strategy of going to large population centers to establish churches which in turn would branch out to other, smaller communities and establish more churches.

FOUNDING OF THE CHURCH

The church began with a reasoned interpretation of Old Testament Messianic passages. "And Paul, as his manner was, went in unto them, and three sabbath days reasoned with them out of the Scriptures, opening and alleging, that Christ must needs have suffered, and risen again from the dead; and that this Jesus, whom I preach unto you, is Christ" (Acts 17:2, 3). St. Paul's approach was based on reason and Scripture.

61

Churches of the New Testament Era: Principles

The result? "And some of them believed, and consorted with Paul and Silas; and of the devout Greeks a great multitude, and of the chief women not a few" (Acts 17:4).

But the enemy was soon at work.

Opposition from envy. "But the Jews which believed not, moved with envy..." (Acts 17:5). "For ye, brethren, became followers of the churches of God which in Judea are in Christ Jesus: for ye also have suffered like things of your own countrymen, even as they have of the Jews" (1 Thessalonians 2:14).

Opposition by force. "But the Jews which believed not, moved with envy, took unto them certain lewd fellows of the baser sort, and gathered a company, and set all the city on an uproar, and assaulted the house of Jason, and sought to bring them out to the people" (Acts 17:5).

The greatest compliment ever given Christianity by its enemies was bestowed here, the unintentional tribute paid these Apostles being: "These that have turned the whole world upside down are come hither also" (Acts 17:6).

Opposition by legal means. Before the magistrates, the accusers charged St. Paul and Silas: "These all do contrary to the decrees of Caesar, saying that there is another king, one Jesus" (Acts 17:7).

Despite the resistance, Paul taught all of the doctrines of the Faith and later addressed two Epistles to the church at Thessalonika. In his personal visits (there were probably others besides the first) and in his two letters, we are able to tell a great deal about the universal principles which emerged here for all the churches thereafter to follow. In fact, some scholars refer to 1 Thessalonians 1:1-4 as a description of the "model church." (See the introduction to 1 Thessalonians in *Scofield Reference Bible*.)

This principle of universal influence is mentioned in 1 Thessalonians 1:7, 8 when St. Paul says of the church: "So that ye were ensamples to all that believe... for from you sounded out the word of the Lord not only in Macedonia and Achaia, but also in every place your faith to God-ward is spread abroad; so that we need not to speak anything."

Many of the Thessalonians who became Christians were Jews;

others were Gentiles. In 1 Thessalonians 1:9, St. Paul describes some members of the congregation as those who "turned to God from idols to serve the living and true God."

THE CHURCH IN CONFLICT

The congregation was a church in conflict from the beginning, as the story in Acts tells us. Later St. Paul wrote the church: "... We were bold in our God to speak unto you the gospel of God with much contention" (1 Thessalonians 2:2).

PRINCIPLES OF APOSTOLIC PREACHING

St. Paul stressed that he spoke the *truth*: "For neither at any time used we flattering words, as ye know, nor a cloak of covetousness ... not as pleasing men, but God, which trieth our hearts" (1 Thessalonians 2:5, 4).

He also stressed his *independence*: " ... laboring night and day, because we would not be chargeable unto any of you" (1 Thessalonians 2:9). He worked to earn his living rather than to be supported by the congregation, thus proving the genuineness of his motives.

APOSTOLIC CARE

Timothy was sent by Paul from Athens to learn whether or not the Thessalonians had remained true to the faith. Upon Timothy's return the Apostle was encouraged to learn that all was well. "For this cause, when I could no longer forbear, I sent to know your faith, lest by some means the tempter have tempted you, and our labor be in vain. But now when Timotheus came from you unto us, and brought us good tidings of your faith and charity, and that ye have good remembrance of us always, desiring greatly to see us, as we also to see you: Therefore, brethren, we were comforted over you in all our affliction and distress by your faith" (1 Thessalonians 3:5-7).

SEXUAL TEMPTATION

Early in the history of the churches, the problem of the sexual licentiousness of the Roman-Greco civilization was challenged by Christian sexual morality based upon the sanctity of sex.

"For this is the will of God, even your sanctification, that ye should abstain from fornication: That every one of you should know how to possess his vessel in sanctification and honor; Not in the lust of concupiscence, even as the Gentiles which know not God: That no man go beyond and defraud his brother in any matter: because that the Lord is the avenger of all such, as we also have forewarned you and testified. For God hath not called us unto uncleanness, but unto holiness" (1 Thessalonians 4:3-7).

THE WORD OF GOD

Early in his ministry St. Paul claimed that his message was veritably the Word of God. Churches still preach St. Paul's writings and teachings as "God's revelation."

"For this cause also thank we God without ceasing, because, when ye received the word of God which ye heard of us, ye received it not as the word of men, but as it is in truth, the word of God, which effectually worketh also in you that believe" (1 Thessalonians 2:13).

"Therefore, brethren, stand fast, and hold the traditions which ye have been taught, whether by word, or our epistle" (2 Thessalonians 2:15).

THE MINISTRY

The Epistles St. Paul wrote were intended to be manuals of instruction. This usage is followed today. The passage where this principle is openly stated is: "I charge you by the Lord, that this epistle be read unto all the holy brethren" (1 Thessalonians 5:27).

There was an order of ministerial leadership in the church. St. Paul spoke of it in 1 Thessalonians 5:12, 13: "And we beseech you, brethren, to know them which labor among you, and are over you in the Lord, and admonish you: And to esteem them very highly in love for their work's sake. And be at peace among yourselves."

PERSECUTION

The churches were taught to expect persecution. The martyrdom which is taking place today in the dictatorships of Ghana, Uganda, and elsewhere, especially in the Communist world, parallel St. Paul's words in 1 Thessalonians 3:3, 4: "That no man should be moved by these afflictions: for yourselves know that we are appointed thereunto. For verily, when we were with you, we told you before that we should suffer tribulation; even as it came to pass, and ye know."

Encouragement was given by St. Paul in 2 Thessalonians 1:4: "So that we ourselves glory in you in the churches of God, for your patience and faith in all your persecutions and tribulations that ye endure."

St. Paul's explanation of the purpose for which persecution is given and the good that may come out of it is still helpful today: "Which is a manifest token of the righteous judgment of God, that ye may be counted worthy of the kingdom of God, for which ye also suffer" (2 Thessalonians 1:5). "That the name of our Lord Jesus Christ may be glorified in you, and ye in him, according to the grace of our God and the Lord Jesus Christ" (2 Thessalonians 1:12).

The doctrine of the Second Coming was emphasized in both Epistles as a part of needed encouragement in the face of persecution. These passages were of great help to both the Thessalonian church and to all churches faced by trouble ever since: "But I would not have you to be ignorant, brethren, concerning them which are asleep, that ye sorrow not, even as others which have no hope. For if we believe that Jesus died and rose again, even so them also which sleep in Jesus will God bring with him" (1 Thessalonians 4:13, 14). "And the Lord direct your hearts into the love of God, and into the patient waiting for Christ" (2 Thessalonians 3:5).

The doctrine of the Second Coming is emphasized more in the Thessalonian letters than any other doctrine and has a distinct influence on the nature of what a church should be; namely, doing all things with the Second Coming in mind.

CHURCH DISCIPLINE

It was inevitable that the human element of disorderly conduct should arise, even in the church of the redeemed. How should the Thessalonian church deal with it, and hence how should churches everywhere cope with such behavior? St. Paul provides the universal principle in 2 Thessalonians 3, within a specific situation; namely, that those who refuse to work should not be supported by the church.

"Now we command you, brethren, in the name of our Lord Jesus Christ, that ye withdraw yourselves from every brother that walketh disorderly, and not 'ter the tradition which he received of us" (vs. 6). "For even w.. en we were with you, this we commanded you, that if any would not work, neither should he eat" (vs. 10). "And if any man obey not our word by this epistle, note that man, and have no company with him, that he may be ashamed" (vs. 14). "Yet account him not as an enemy, but admonish him as a brother" (vs. 15).

The Thessalonian church was a church in need of comfort because of false doctrine concerning the Second Coming, distorted ideas which had confused and dispirited the believers there. It also needed the warning of the Coming of Christ for the reminder that Christians will be held accountable for their works as Christians at the *bema* or judgment seat of Christ. He will judge them at the time of His return to gather His own out of this world at the time of the first resurrection.

Eight
BEREA

Sometimes spelled Boerea, and in modern Greek Verria, this was in St. Paul's day, and is in ours, what we would call a "county seat." It was on the great highway which led from Antioch westward toward Rome, cutting across the northern section of the Grecian peninsula to the Adriatic Sea. It was and is essentially a trading city for a fertile area of Greece. The land is rich, and farms are found in abundance. Life there was, and is, without sophistication and had a certain integrity which we associate with the soil and honest manual labor.

In the first century, there was a Jewish synagogue there, to which St. Paul and his party were brought by Christians who accompanied them from Thessalonika.

St. Paul, Timothy, and Silas went into the synagogue to open the Scriptures to the congregation of Jews and Greek proselytes, including men and women of both races.

St. Paul was pleasantly surprised at their reception. The congregation was without antagonism and gave due heed to what he preached to them. He probably presented expositions from the Old Testament Scriptures, as he had in Thessalonika; that is, he read Messianic passages and applied their fulfillment to Jesus.

The threefold response of the people in Berea set forth a pattern for all churches to emulate. Christian churches ever since have been willing to cite the example of the people in Berea as the proper way for all who sincerely wish to find and do the will of God.

OPEN MINDS

"These were more noble than those in Thessalonica, in that they received the word with all *readiness of mind*, and searched the Scriptures daily, whether those things were so" (Acts 17:11).

Closed minds can frustrate the intentions of God. Moreover, closed minds indicate a sinful unwillingness to know more about God and His purposes.

OPEN BIBLE

These people wanted to learn spiritual truth from the highest authority, and therefore went to the Scriptures as their only rule for faith and practice. They were willing to let the Scriptures decide. They did not, of course, possess a single book of the New Testament; but there was sufficient evidence in the Old Testament Scriptures, which they did have, to convince them that Jesus was the Messiah.

OPEN HEARTS

Having seen the truth, they were willing to commit themselves to it. This is the acid test of the open mind and the sincere quest for truth. Without personal commitment, truth newly understood is only an intellectual assent. To become a believer, surrendered to Christ as Lord, is the thing that counts. This is why church membership is the natural outcome of faith professed.

We never read further in the Book of Acts or in the Epistles about the church of Berea, but we shall never hear the end of its influence. After the vengeful, unbelieving Jews of Thessalonika arrived on the scene to create a public uproar, Timothy and Silas remained in Berea for a few weeks to further instruct the believers there, while St. Paul was escorted by members of the church away from the city and to Athens. Later Timothy and Silas joined St. Paul in Corinth, far to the south. But the story in the Book of Acts about the believers in Berea would probably not have been recorded had the Bereans not continued in the faith.

Nine
ATHENS

The founding of the church at Athens has been overshadowed by the record which St. Luke gives of the magnificent *apologia* (i.e., presentation or defense) of the Gospel by St. Paul before the council of philosophers on Mars' Hill. Nevertheless, a church *was* founded, and the day came when Christianity became a strong force throughout Greece.

The Areopagus, the council before whom St. Paul appeared for questioning, probably included the city's intellectual elite and certainly the ruling element of the state. Evidently membership in this group was eagerly sought and quite exclusive. Its members were men who had enough time, money, and intellectual curiosity to debate philosophy in Athens, the "home of philosophy."

Long before the first century, such famous names as Plato, Aristotle, and Socrates were associated with Athens. To this day, the intellectual disciplines and approaches of the philosophers of ancient Athens are considered foundational in philosophical circles. At many times during subsequent history—even in the history of Christianity—the logic and often the ethical conclusions of the philosophers of Athens have been very influential among some theologians and thinkers. The insights of Aristotle were very persuasive and considered by many to be of great value.

THE LIMITATIONS OF PHILOSOPHY

Athenian philosophy suffered from three defects: It was born (and flourished) in a *pagan* (idol-worshiping) setting. It depended upon *reason* rather than experimentation; hence, it was prescientific, speculative, and not fully able to check its ideas

69

against the world as it really was. It was *ignorant of divine revelation*; hence, it could not know much about the true goals of human existence as revealed in the Bible.

Athenian philosophy, led by master thinkers, had laid the groundwork for psychology and philosophy as they are taught today. But in Paul's time it could not seem to shake off the superstition of idolatry and the limited world view of the first century. There were no famous philosophers in Athens then. Those who met in the Areopagus were speculative dilettantes who fancied themselves as the inheritors of the great Greek minds of the past. Actually, they were mere rehashers, and they added nothing to the conclusions or methods discovered four centuries before in the golden age of Athenian philosophy. Nevertheless, they kept the tradition of philosophical speculation alive, and possessed some legal power to protect the worship of the gods and preserve public order.

It was before this body, the Areopagus, that St. Paul appeared, upon their members' demand, to explain about the two strange gods of whom (they thought) he spoke. "Tell us about Jesus and Anastasis," they said, supposing that *anastasis* (the Greek word for resurrection) was a god. They were in for a surprise.

CHRISTIANITY vs. CLASSICAL PHILOSOPHY

St. Luke does not assign a long time to St. Paul's stay in Athens. Perhaps it was at most a month. The reason Athens was important to the writer of Acts, and to us, is that we can learn much from Paul's presentation of the Gospel to the intellectual and philosophical world of his time.

Here Christianity came into a spiritual confrontation with pagan, philosophical Athens. This was a classic example of St. Paul's missionary methods—what he did and what he did not do—and revealed the way this great Christian thinker presented Christianity to philosophers.

A word is in order at this point to those of the Christian faith today who may confront the contentions of modern philosophers, who with all their intellectual brilliance are yet unable to come to agreement in presenting a workable, unified plan and purpose for living.

70

Athens

Present-day philosophy is more disciplined by science, more able to extend the horizons of knowledge; but like its counterpart in ancient Athens, it still seems impotent to help people. It may have improved its diagnosis, but the cure is as far away today as it was in the first century.

Philosophy is useful because it is broadening, and it puts logic in its proper place as an important tool of knowledge. But philosophy cannot redeem, cannot satisfy; man cannot by reason alone discover the meaning and purpose of life. With that fact in mind, it is instructive to note that in Athens Christianity met philosophy on its own home ground, and that it still can and must do so today.

St. Paul's experience is relevant to the present. The story in Acts 17:16-34 is not so much the story of a local New Testament era church working out universal principles, as it is that of a Christian missionary, himself an intellectual, who challenged philosophers to become Christian believers.

"Now while Paul waited for them at Athens, his spirit was stirred in him, when he saw the city wholly given to idolatry. Therefore disputed he in the synagogue with the Jews, and with the devout persons, and in the market daily with them that met with him. Then certain philosophers of the Epicureans, and of the Stoics, encountered him. And some said, What will this babbler say? other some, He seemeth to be a setter forth of strange gods: because he preached unto them Jesus, and the resurrection.

"And they took him, and brought him unto Areopagus, saying, May we know what this new doctrine, whereof thou speakest, is? For thou bringest certain strange things to our ears: we would know therefore what these things mean. (For all the Athenians, and strangers which were there, spent their time in nothing else, but either to tell or to hear some new thing.)

"Then Paul stood in the midst of Mars' hill, and said, Ye men of Athens, I perceive that in all things ye are too superstitious. For as I passed by, and beheld your devotions, I found an altar with this inscription, TO THE UNKNOWN GOD. Whom therefore ye ignorantly worship, him declare I unto you. God that made the world and all things therein, seeing that he is Lord of heaven and earth, dwelleth not in temples made with hands;

71

Churches of the New Testament Era: Principles

Neither is worshipped with men's hands, as though he needed any thing, seeing he giveth to all life, and breath, and all things; And hath made of one blood all nations of men for to dwell on all the face of the earth, and hath determined the times before appointed, and the bounds of their habitation; That they should seek the Lord, if haply they might feel after him, and find him, though he be not far from every one of us: For in him we live, and move, and have our being; as certain also of your own poets have said, For we are also his offspring. Forasmuch then as we are the offspring of God, we ought not to think that the Godhead is like unto gold, or silver, or stone, graven by art and man's device. And the times of this ignorance God winked at; but now commandeth all men everywhere to repent: Because he hath appointed a day, in the which he will judge the world in righteousness by that man whom he hath ordained; whereof he hath given assurance unto all men, in that he hath raised him from the dead.

"And when they heard of the resurrection of the dead, some mocked: and others said, We will hear thee again of this matter. So Paul departed from among them. Howbeit certain men clave unto him, and believed: among the which was Dionysius the Areopagite, and a woman named Damaris, and others with them."

Out of this a church was formed. Perhaps the chief principle which came forth from the founding of the church at Athens was this: *Christianity demands that man go further than philosophy can take him*.

The Areopagus was divided into several schools of thought, but the largest division was between the Epicureans and the Stoics. The Epicureans stressed wise decisions, so that in the end pleasure might be the supreme consequence. The Stoics believed in overcoming the desire for pleasure, so virtue could triumph.

St. Paul was certainly more favorable toward the morally superior Stoics. In fact, he quoted one of their poets in his message, in which their three principles were given: love to man; reverence to the gods; purity of self. However, he ignored the philosophy of the Epicureans who taught, "Eat, drink, and be merry, for tomorrow you may die." He disagreed with the

Stoics' view that nothing lies beyond death except the reabsorbing of human life into the "great cosmic consciousness." St. Paul had the resurrection of Jesus to proclaim, which contradicted both these great Athenian schools of philosophy. St. Paul provided a truer goal for living: to seek and to do the will of the living Creator who will someday judge all men in regard to sin and righteousness.

Both philosophies in Athens were skeptically religious. To the Epicurean, religion was merely a means to greater wisdom for living here and now. For both, religion ended at the grave. The Stoics were pantheists who thought each god was a part of the God. The Epicureans were more agnostic in their ideas of deity, believing the gods to be beyond reach or knowledge.

THE NATURE OF PRESENT-DAY PHILOSOPHICAL RELIGION

Certain religious cults today draw much from the Epicurean and the Stoic traditions, although perhaps unconsciously. They are vague and agnostic about the afterlife, maintaining that at death the human spirit returns to the cosmic life force of the universe. They deny a personal God. They are primarily concerned with living this present life more easily, more masterfully, and more positively. In a sense, like the Athenians, these cults, though not guilty of social evils or personal debauchery, are this-life-oriented. They are, in other words, ethical only because kindness, altruism, and positive thinking are in the long run more pleasurable.

The Christian church today must confront this philosophy. And the cults do espouse philosophy, not religion or Christian theology. Their congregations may call themselves "churches," perhaps for tax reasons. But these cults are only philosophies of living, not theologically oriented religions or church bodies. Our laws in America do not distinguish between a theological religion and an ethical philosophical group, and most people do not know the difference.

Yet the church must confront this growing perversion of religion. The cults must be shown for what they are, an ethical (in

73

one sense) substitute for genuine religion. The philosophical approach may have religious overtones, but it is not God-centered. Such philosophical "religion" has penetrated beyond the cults into liberal churches and is very widespread today.

The main problem with Athenian philosophy was that in the *name* of religion it denied *true* religion. "What concord hath Athens with Jerusalem?" cried one early Christian thinker, the great Tertullian, for he saw that the two approaches are never the same. No matter how many "gods" Athens had, it featured a philosophy of ethics and an "art of living" that was not a faith in God.

It is an exercise in insight to see how little theology and how much present-life philosophy appears in many churches today. St. Paul would think himself back in Athens were he to come to Los Angeles, although the marble idols would be few and a greater sophistication would be evident in this present-day presentation of Epicurean and Stoic philosophies.

To demonstrate the relevance of the founding of the church at Athens, the reader is invited to look at the titles of "sermons" listed by cults in a 1977 Los Angeles Saturday church advertisement page. They reveal no Gospel, only a philosophical presentation of the art of better living. God, the reader will note, is still "unknown" to these people if one were to draw conclusions from these sermon themes:

> Passing Life's Tests
> An Exercise in Meditation
> Possibility vs. Probability
> Teaching the Art of Living
> The Power Within You
> Welcome to Your World
> Conformity and Rebellion and Something in Between
> How to Develop Cosmic Knowledge
> Creative Self-identity
> The Delights of the Inner Path
> Delights and Surprises along the Path
> It Is Natural for You to Have Radiant Health
> I Will Not Fear
> The Art of Being Creative

Athens

Live This Day Wholly Now
Being, Where You Are
The Way to Emotional Health
Daily Use of Science of Mind
The Healing Power of Light and Color
Mind Is the Master Weaver

These are only some of the sermon or lesson topics heard on the Sunday being advertised. What conclusions can be drawn?

1. *These are simply modern restatements of the Epicurean and Stoic philosophies*. They do not embrace Christian theology, although some Scripture passages were perhaps quoted to give a Christian flavor to naturalistic philosophy.

2. *These groups are not churches in the New Testament sense*, but are philosophical study groups.

3. Their messages have little to do with the Christ of the Bible, the nature of God, the destiny of man, sin, and salvation. They speak about ethics, but without bringing in God's absolute standards of right and wrong.

4. *These messages are "you"-centered*, pleasure-oriented, involved with this life only, and indifferent to the demands of God and the Bible, except to use such texts as would seem to give biblical support. Indeed, there is no true exposition of the Bible in these groups. In fact, they attempt to spiritualize the Bible as much as possible, taking biblical events and history to have only a parabolic authority. Nothing in the message of Christ and the Apostles is to be taken at face value, but only as symbolic, as an illustration of ethical or pragmatic principles. "This" stands for "that," and one is not to be concerned with biblical theology. If and when it contradicts what their philosophies may teach, their views are to take precedence.

Interestingly, the problems of textual research and biblical scholarship have no importance for these cultists. The principles of *hermeneutics* are unknown. The preaching of the cross, so beloved by St. Paul, is beyond their interest or concern. The bodily resurrection is not relevant, and a final judgment is preposterous.

This is what existentialist ideas stress: concern with the here and now; the use of the "laws of life" to gain earthly pleasure and success. "God," who to most such philosophers is not really personal but a name for a nonpersonal Creative Force (which is an impossibility), becomes man's servant. God is to them a cosmic, invisible bellboy to carry out their wishes when they learn how to press the buttons correctly. The message of all these cults is: "Discover the powers of the universe within yourself and use them to be happy." So it was in ancient Athens!

In contrast, Christianity teaches that man is God's servant, not God's master. If man will not eventually say to God, "Thy will be done," God will someday, reluctantly, forever turn away from rebellious man and say with sorrowful finality, "*thy* will be done!"

ST. PAUL vs. ATHENIAN PHILOSOPHY

Paul's confrontation on Mars' Hill resulted in a Christian church in Athens. This would not have happened if St. Paul had not been willing to demonstrate the difference between the divine revelation of the risen historic Jesus Christ and the ignorance and emptiness of the philosophical "religion" of the Epicureans and Stoics. Hence, the church in Athens represents the triumph of the Christian Faith over the philosophical "this life only" approach of the Areopagus. The church today must follow the universally applicable principles of such a witness as used by St. Paul in Athens.

ST. PAUL'S APPROACH

1. *St. Paul paid respectful recognition to the existence and widespread prevalence of the religious symbolism of the Athenians*. The Parthenon, with all its beauty and the countless idols erected to every god imaginable, was before him as he spoke.

"Now while Paul waited for them at Athens, his spirit was stirred in him, when he saw the city wholly given to idolatry" (17:16). "Then Paul stood in the midst of Mars' hill, and said, Ye men of Athens, I perceive that in all things ye are too superstitious. For as I passed by, and beheld your devotions, I found an altar with this inscription, TO THE UNKNOWN GOD. Whom therefore ye ignorantly worship, him declare I unto you. God that made the world and all things therein, seeing that he is Lord of heaven and earth, dwelleth not in temples made with hands. . . . For in him we live, and move, and have our being; as certain also of your own poets have said, For we are also his offspring" (17:22-24, 28).

2. *Idolatry*, which was then the visible manifestation of both ignorance and a "this life only" approach, *is evil and must be abandoned*, said St. Paul. "At the times of this ignorance God winked at; but now commandeth all men every where to repent" (17:30).

The word "repent" means little unless there is the realization that the philosophical approach is both inadequate and sinful.

3. The reason their ignorance will no longer serve as an excuse, said St. Paul, involves *the certainty of a final judgment by Jesus Christ*. Christ had been certified by God, by reason of His bodily resurrection, to be the One to judge mankind concerning righteousness or lack of it.

"Because he hath appointed a day, in the which he will judge the world in righteousness by that man whom he hath ordained; whereof he hath given assurance unto all men, in that he hath raised him from the dead" (17:31).

Idolatry in Athens was only a mask for more subtle evils—the philosophical worship of the state and of personal pleasure. This was the substantive meaning of the philosophical approach of that day. Today's idols are not usually called "idols." But in the sense that things rule people and limit their concerns to "this life only," "idols" are still worshiped (that is, given supreme devotion). The Athenian figures of marble, gold, and silver were only the outward manifestation of a desire on the part of the worshiper to bend the forces of life to his own welfare. Then and now, this is not good enough. Man needs more than himself, more than insights for the art of living.

God demands repentance from our self-centeredness and from our preoccupation with our own concerns. "He hath set eternity in our hearts." In view of the authority of the risen Christ, we ought to yield to God's eternal purposes, for judgment is ahead!

The little "self-help realizations" and "art-of-living" philosophies may (some of them) be all right in their place, but they should not be central. When we crowd God out and place self on the throne, we have missed the purpose for which God created us (Acts 17:28). We should seek the Lord and find Him and His purposes, said St. Paul: "That they should seek the Lord, if haply they might feel after him, and find him, though he be not far from every one of us" (17:27).

THE CHURCH IN ATHENS

What a defeat for Christianity it would have been if no one had responded to St. Paul's profound witness before the council of philosophers. Indeed, some, if not most, scoffed at the resurrection message. Yet a church *was* formed.

"Howbeit certain men clave unto him, and believed: among the which was Dionysius the Areopagite, and a woman named Damaris, and others with them" (17:34).

These were the people, including Dionysius, a member of the Areopagus, who became the first members of the church. Now *they* talked about Christ, and their witness bore fruit. In time the Areopagus disappeared, and Athens became a great center of worldwide Christian influence. Today Greece is nominally Christian, the headquarters of a great branch of organized Christianity. In downtown Athens, there is a very large cathedral which stands in memory of St. Paul's brief visit. It is called The Church of St. Dionysius, the Areopagite.

But, of course, the really significant church principle which came out of the early church in Athens lies in the approach St. Paul used in its founding. This is needed by churches today: we must confront substitutes for religion with this truth—the heart of spiritual life is surrender to God and His purposes for life. We are not to be content with superstitions, empty religious ceremonies, efforts to bend the gods (the principles of positive thinking, etc.) to our comfort and pleasures; or with philosophy in its vain and empty deceits, a poor counterfeit of a real faith in the living Christ.

We cannot find the meaning of life merely by looking for it through any kind of human philosophy. But we can allow God to find us and to reveal to us His secret of life, which is "to glorify God and enjoy Him forever"!

Ten
CORINTH

St. Paul came to Corinth alone, and there told Jews and Greeks in the local synagogue that Jesus was the Messiah. He soon had as his helpers Aquila and Priscilla, who had been expelled from Rome by Claudius because they were Jews. St. Paul met them in the manufacturing district of Corinth, where he went to work to support himself as a tentmaker. This devoted couple were ardent Christians and served with St. Paul not only in Corinth, but later in Ephesus and elsewhere. Spiritually mature, they showed a quick and profound grasp of the essentials of the Gospel, and later instructed such luminaries as Apollos, a gifted Jewish convert from Alexandria who became a noted Christian evangelist.

It is evident that Priscilla and her husband Aquila were both adept in the art of Christian instruction. Together, they were a formidable team for Christ. They moved about in their ministry and later returned to Rome. In his Epistle to the Romans, St. Paul speaks of them as "my helpers": "Greet Priscilla and Aquila, my helpers in Christ Jesus: Who have for my life laid down their own necks: unto whom not only I give thanks, but also all the churches of the Gentiles" (Romans 16:3, 4).

Upon the arrival of Timothy and Silas from Berea, St. Paul intensified his plea for the Jews of Corinth to turn to Christ. Some did; others blasphemed the Savior. So Paul departed from the synagogue and moved into a house next door. Crispus, the president of the synagogue, went along with St. Paul. Many of the Corinthians were baptized, and a flourishing church was soon underway.

Preparing the Apostle for the trouble which was looming, God appeared to him in a vision with this encouragement: "Be

79

not afraid, but speak, and hold not thy peace:... For I have much people in this city" (Acts 18:9, 10).

THE CITY OF CORINTH

Paul continued a year and six months in this gateway to southern Greece. The city itself was a commercial town where traffic from north to south passed by, and where sea traffic from east to west unloaded and then transshipped cargo over the narrow four-mile isthmus, thus saving many days of shipping time. As a consequence of this traffic, Corinth was large in population and rich in commercial profit, catering to a multitude of strangers with both food and entertainment.

Like all port cities and commercial towns, Corinth was the scene of much immorality. The taverns (as revealed by the archaeologists) were numerous, and prostitution was rampant. The pagan temple on the top of a nearby mountain (Acro-Corinth) housed temple prostitutes whose trade enriched the temple. The word "Corinthian" became a synonym for a person who lives a corrupt sexual existence.

Corinth was a Roman city in a Greek setting, and its wealth made possible much civic improvement. Running water was piped into homes and businesses. The rapid population turnover made it an ideal place to reach many for Christ in all of southern Greece. And God's Word bore much fruit among the commercial travelers who passed through by land and sea.

SPIRITUAL OPPOSITION

Opposition to the Gospel came from Jews who did not believe. Charges were laid against St. Paul before Gallio, the Roman deputy, at the civil court (the *bema* or judgment seat), a building which is still visible today. Gallio recognized the religious character of the dispute, involving the Jews and Christians. He swiftly had Sosthenes, the new president of the synagogue, beaten, and then he dismissed the crowd.

After the disturbance, St. Paul remained for quite some time and then sailed to Syria by way of Ephesus, taking Aquila and Priscilla with him. Later he returned to Corinth, and wrote the Epistle to the Romans while there.

UNIVERSAL CHURCH PRINCIPLES
EVIDENT IN CORINTH

We are fortunate to have not only a lengthy account in the Book of Acts about St. Paul and the Corinthian church, but also substantial commentary on that church in First and Second Corinthians. We have vastly more information about the inner workings of that church, as the Gospel confronted Jews, proselytes, pagans, civil authorities, and a transient population, than about any other church of the New Testament era.

The very length of time St. Paul spent there (at least two years, counting his several visits) and the letters written there to other churches, plus those which were written to the Corinthian church itself, reveal many insights and provide a wealth of information in our search for the true nature of the early church.

The first Epistle to the Corinthian church was prompted by a delegation which came to St. Paul in Ephesus, detailing ten major problems which had brought much trouble to the congregation in Corinth. The second epistle was in response to the rumors which reached St. Paul that the reception of the first epistle had been cool and that St. Paul himself had been accused of not being an authentic Apostle. This cast doubts on his proposed mission of mercy to take funds to Jerusalem after they were collected by the congregation in Corinth.

The way in which St. Paul treated these many problems reveals a great deal about the policies of the church in the first century. These policies became widely adopted and are still considered important for churches today.

1. *Party spirit condemned*. From the outset of its turbulent life, the church at Corinth was prone to divisions and factionalism. "There are contentions among you," said Paul, and noted that the believers had chosen leaders with whom they identified in a superior spirit. St. Paul's answer to carnality was the Lordship of Christ (1 Corinthians 1:10-12). He reminded his readers that all they had was a gift of God; hence, they had no reason to be puffed up and proud (4:7).

2. *The social makeup of the church was unimportant*. "God hath chosen the weak things of the world to confound the things which are mighty," said St. Paul (1:26). Not many mighty,

Churches of the New Testament Era: Principles

noble, or wise by human standards made up the flock. The great ability of the early church in Corinth to do God's work through ordinary people became a part of the remarkable power of primitive Christianity wherever it went. This power still belongs to churches which attempt to follow the patterns of the early churches. The members are urged to have the same care one for another (12:25).

3. *The principle of stewardship*. The Christian responsibility of handling money, which, St. Paul taught, given by God to His servants in trust, would be obscure if we did not have the Corinthian letters. St. Paul's teaching and the believers' acceptance of it placed the principles of stewardship firmly in the Corinthian church and all churches since which accept the New Testament concept of the church (4:1-2).

4. *Social purity*. In the midst of shocking immorality, St. Paul enjoined the Corinthian church to discipline their church members who were not willing to forsake social impurity. Exclusion from the fellowship of the church was to be a church matter for disciplining the unrepentant (5:11).

However, the repentant were to be forgiven and restored (2 Corinthians 2:6, 7).

5. *The church members were to judge their own quarrels*. An early church principle frequently violated today was expressed by St. Paul, "Dare any of you . . . go to law before the unjust, and not before the saints?" (1 Corinthians 6:1, 2). Present-day Christians should take this principle more seriously, lest the cause of Christ be hurt.

6. *Christian liberty*. St. Paul recognized the obvious truth that meat is just food. In that day, it was usually available cheaply in the temple of the pagans where, as a consequence of animal sacrifice, it was sold in abundance. The problem was that Christians purchasing it might be construed as being secretly devoted to idols. Therefore, St. Paul explained the need to avoid the appearance of evil, not because of the meat but because of the Christian's potentially harmful influence on weaker brethren (8:9). Idols represented demons, declared St. Paul (10:20). Christians were forbidden to knowingly eat meat declared to be sacrificed to idols, if this would make another stumble (10:27-29).

7. *The ministry and the church*. St. Paul set forth for all time

the principle that the ministers of the church have a right to be supported by the church (9:7-14). But the Apostle himself did did avail himself of this right (9:15).

8. *Conduct at the Lord's Supper*. Evidently the Lord's Supper (called "communion" by St. Paul in 10:16) was universally observed by the early churches. Yet it was only to the Corinthian church that any apostolic instruction was written. Here the Apostle urged self-judgment before partaking of the symbols of God's forgiveness. He also urged people to avoid excess in the love feast which preceded the communion service.

9. *The standard of Christian behavior*. The teaching of Jesus about "turning the other cheek" was amplified into a behavioral code by St. Paul to cover many situations confronted within the church by its members: "Give none offense, neither to the Jews, nor to the Gentiles, nor to the church of God" (10:32).

10. *Spiritual gifts*. Certain abilities, useful to the work of the church, given by the Holy Spirit to believers, are explained by St. Paul. The list is found in 12:8-10. Further, God sets some in the church with special callings. This list is found in 12:28, 29. Churches everywhere can find these gifts and callings if they are claimed. Perhaps the lack of power and effectiveness in many churches is due to a failure to appropriate what the Holy Spirit has done for the church and its members. Preaching is said to be the most desirable gift, but it and all gifts are to be administered in love (14:1; 13:1, 2).

11. *Congregational deportment and order in the church*. When the congregation met for services in the early days of Christianity, there was a great deal of freedom on the part of the members. Lacking the New Testament, the members frequently engaged in activities as they felt led. St. Paul urged that this be disciplined by the simple principle of "what edifies?" (14:26-33). While women were not discriminated against in the church, they were urged not to speak "with authority" in the church meetings. This is the Greek meaning of 14:35.

Speaking in "tongues," languages which were special gifts of the Holy Spirit given to help spread the Gospel among people of foreign speech, was always to be accompanied by an interpretation (i.e., translation) when used in the church or not be allowed (14:13-28). (It must be noted that the word "unknown" is not found in the Greek. It is implied in the sense of speech being not understood or being unfamiliar, not in the sense of being unknowable.)

12. *Church work*. Any work done for Christ by His people in the church is worthwhile (15:58).

13. *Offerings*. St. Paul stressed the necessity for the giving of offerings and the practice of stewardship in the church, and also mentioned the principle of regularity (16:1-3). He cites the promise of God to bless the giver (2 Corinthians 9:8-10). He also mentioned the principle of proportionate giving (1 Corinthians 16:2).

14. *False apostles*. Even in the early days of Christianity, there were false Apostles who took advantage of the gullibility and innocence of hospitable church members who characteristically welcomed anyone who claimed to be a brother in Christ. St. Paul described such pretenders in 2 Corinthians 11:4, 13-15.

The church was urged to know and to be able to recognize such false Apostles by their preaching of another Christ, another gospel, another spirit (i.e., an unchristian attitude). Unbelievers of any sort were not to be granted permanent relationships with God's people (6:14-17).

POSTSCRIPT

Toward the end of the first century, Clement, a leader of the churches in Rome, wrote an epistle to the congregation in Corinth. It has come down to us as a valuable first-century document which tells of the eventual *denouement* of the same congregation to which St. Paul had addressed those of his letters which we call First and Second Corinthians.

Alas, according to Clement, the church at the end of the century was still divided, still quarreling, still carnal. How nice it would be to be able to write a happier ending to the story of this church. It had a great deal going for it at its beginning. It had the high honor of being itself the first recipient of no less than two of the major books of the Bible. It was from Corinth that St. Paul wrote the greatest epistle of them all—Romans—as well as First and Second Thessalonians. The Corinthian Church had been started by St. Paul, and had been visited by great preach-

Corinth

ers such as St. Peter and Apollos. In Christian terms, this was indeed a "head start" program!

Yet the church at Corinth was made up of flawed human beings with all the usual foibles and penchants for sinfulness. In brief, the congregation at Corinth was similiar to our churches today. Perhaps we expected too much from its glorious beginnings. There seems to be no way to inoculate any church so that its members cannot weaken or play the fool.

It may, in fact, be a bit comforting to be reminded that our earliest Christian ancestors were no more heroic, nor any wiser than average church members of the present. We dare not be self-righteous when we consider the Corinthian believers. How well do *we* behave when the preaching of the Word in our churches comes through as plainly as it did in Corinth? We had better face the truth that we possess more Scripture than they did—namely, the entire New Testament. We have a multitude of church programs, superb physical facilities in our churches, and Bibles for everyone. The Corinthians had much less to work with.

It seems strange that we expect a higher level of Christian behavior and better solutions to church problems from the Corinthian believers than we expect of ourselves today. So we are disappointed when we find out they were so like us.

There was nothing about living in what *we* call the early church era that made people more saintly than at later times. In those days, the Gospel rebuked sins and Christ produced some godly people. Yet into the same church came others who remained cantankerous, petty, fleshly minded, proud, and given to a party spirit; all this despite the presence in their midst of the Apostles' mighty ministry. The situation was as St. Paul had said to them: "we have this treasure in earthen vessels, that the excellency of the power may be of God, and not of us" (2 Corinthians 4:7).

The marvel is not that through the ages the church has survived its enemies, but that it has survived its members. That too is a universal principle we can learn from our search for the early church in Corinth.

Ephesus: city of the Apostles Paul, John, and Timothy.

Eleven
EPHESUS

We learn a great deal about the church at Ephesus from a lengthy passage in Acts 19 and also from the Epistle to the Ephesians, where fifteen universal church principles are set forth.

The Epistle to the Ephesians was written in Rome while St. Paul was in prison, and probably was sent to Ephesus along with the Epistle to the Colossians, the Epistle to Philemon, and a lost letter to the Laodiceans.

These letters were carried by Tychicus, a minister, and Onesimus, an escaped slave who belonged to Philemon and who had fled to Rome where he was led to Christ by St. Paul. He willingly returned to his master, bearing the delightful Epistle to Philemon in which St. Paul interceded for the runaway slave.

Because there are no personal greetings for specific individuals in the Ephesian letter, some have claimed that St. Paul did not address the letter to the Ephesian church at all. Some have thought that the Epistle to the Ephesians was actually the lost letter to the Laodiceans mentioned in the Epistle to the Colossians: "And when this epistle is read among you, cause that it be read also in the church of the Laodiceans; and that ye likewise read the epistle from Laodicea" (Colossians 4:16). But this is doubtful. It may well be that St. Paul wrote Ephesians with a view to its also being circulated to other churches. Nevertheless, it seems to have been addressed primarily to that one church. We are not sure St. Paul ever wrote "circular letters," though it is plain he intended more than one congregation to read most of them.

The Acts 19 account of the founding of the church in Ephesus is rich with detail. St. Paul saw that this seaport city was a hub where highways converged from all over the province of Asia.

In later Christian history, the church at Ephesus became large and powerful. In fact, under St. Paul's ministry the Ephesian church grew to such proportions that, despite opposition from unbelieving Jews and idol-making silversmiths, great numbers of converts made a clear break with superstition and paganism by burning their books of magic and astrology.

Much later, St. John made Ephesus his headquarters, and upon his death was buried there. His tomb is overshadowed by the ruins of a great church building dating from the fifth century. Other large church building ruins are found in Ephesus, which after Antioch was the most important Christian city in the world until the Roman church became prominent. Great church councils were held here in the stormy days of the rise of the Byzantine churches. The patriarchate was moved to Constantinople early in the fourth century when the headquarters of the Roman Empire also was transferred there.

Ephesus remained an important church center for centuries until it was gradually abandoned because of earthquakes, the silting of the harbor, the rise of the nearby and better port of Smyrna, and its eventual and final destruction in A.D. 1453 by the Turks. By then history had relegated Ephesus to the past. Today a small Turkish farm town occupies a nearby site, but no living congregation of Christians can be found.

CHURCH PRINCIPLES LEARNED FROM EPHESUS

1. *The correct meaning of Christian baptism*: There were proto-Christians in Ephesus who had been baptized by John the Baptist, or perhaps by John's followers. This baptism showed a spirit of repentance. They were right toward God in attitude, but knew nothing of the Holy Spirit and the fullness of the Christian message. After instruction by St. Paul, these believers were rebaptized to symbolize their acceptance of the meaning of Christian baptism (faith in the living, risen Jesus Christ). John's baptism could be considered a negative baptism, a sign of repentance of and turning away from sin. Christian baptism is an

affirmation of positive faith in Christ. The obvious lesson is that just any baptism is not sufficient. Baptism, to be meaningful, must reflect the believer's faith in the risen Christ for salvation.

2. *The church congregated in a large, rented building.* It is quite astonishing to learn that the Christians of the first two centuries used homes and schools as meeting places. They didn't have their own buildings for Christian worship, however needed, until the end of the second century. "But when divers were hardened, and believed not, but spake evil of that way before the multitude, he departed from them, and separated the disciples, disputing daily in the school of one Tyrannus. And this continued by the space of two years; so that all they which dwelt in Asia heard the word of the Lord Jesus, both Jews and Greeks" (Acts 19:9, 10). The lesson is that while church buildings are useful, they are not absolutely necessary to the existence of a church.

3. *Church members publicly severed themselves from their past superstitions.* "That if thou shalt confess with thy mouth the Lord Jesus, and shalt believe in thine heart that God hath raised him from the dead, thou shalt be saved" (Romans 10:9).

This verse declares that a *public* profession of faith accompanies salvation. In Ephesus the new believers, turning in great numbers to Christ, held a public renouncement ceremony by burning their books of magic and witchcraft. The principle revealed here is that secret believers are not fully Christian until they take a public stand for Christ, renouncing their old superstitions or allegiances.

4. *The head of the congregation is Jesus Christ, regardless of who may be elected as the human leader or leaders.* The church, in the plan of God, is a monarchy, a democracy, and a republic. Christ is King; hence, the church is a monarchy. The people have a voice in decisions and policies; hence, the church is a democracy. Church leaders are elected or appointed for a time; thus, the church is a republic. The church has three forms of government, depending upon the given situation. But Christ rules! " . . . And hath put all things under his feet, and gave him to be the head over all things to the church" (Ephesians 1:22).

5. *The congregation is not to maintain a wall of distinction be-*

tween its members. "For he is our peace, who hath made both one, and hath broken down the middle wall of partition between us" (2:14).

6. *Jesus Christ is the foundation and chief cornerstone of the church*. The teachings of the Apostles and prophets about Christ are also part of this foundation: "And are built upon the foundation of the apostles and prophets, Jesus Christ himself being the chief corner stone" (2:20).

7. *The congregation is fully inhabited by the living presence of the Holy Spirit*. "In whom ye also are builded together for a habitation of God through the Spirit" (2:22).

8. *The church is to be a treasury of spiritual knowledge*. "To the intent that now unto the principalities and powers in heavenly places might be known by the church the manifold wisdom of God" (3:10).

9. *The church exists to bring glory to God*. "Unto him be glory in the church by Christ Jesus throughout all ages, world without end. Amen" (3:21).

10. *The unity of the congregation is to reflect the unity of the Godhead*. "Endeavouring to keep the unity of the Spirit in the bond of peace. There is one body, and one Spirit, even as ye are called in one hope of your calling; One Lord, one faith, one baptism" (4:3-5).

11. *All church officials' primary responsibility is to build up the congregation*. That is, their offices are bestowed not for display or for personal attention, but for building up the membership and the spiritual stature of the members. "Till we all come in the unity of the faith, and of the knowledge of the Son of God, unto a perfect man, unto the measure of the stature of the fulness of Christ" (4:13).

12. *The musical program of the church should encourage the membership and give glory to God*. "Speaking to yourselves in psalms and hymns and spiritual songs, singing and making melody in your heart to the Lord; Giving thanks always for all things unto God and the Father in the name of our Lord Jesus Christ" (5:19, 20).

13. *The attitude of Jesus Christ toward His church*: If people love Jesus, they will love what He loved and, like Him, "give themselves for it." Ephesians 5 is perhaps the most important moti-

vational passage on the church in the entire New Testament. It is in sad contrast to the widespread neglect and lack of affection for the church which is seen today among so many Christians who consider the church merely a place to worship. "Husbands, love your wives, even as Christ also loved the church, and gave himself for it" (5:25). "For no man ever yet hated his own flesh; but nourisheth and cherisheth it, even as the Lord the church" (5:29).

There are in these passages four statements about Christ's love for the congregation which bears His name: He loved it. He gave Himself for it. He nourishes it. He cherishes it.

14. *Born-again church members are also members of His body.* They are now members of the local assembly and, in prospect, members of His "general assembly" when it becomes His "body" and "bride" at His second coming. "For we are members of his body, of his flesh, and of his bones. For this cause shall a man leave his father and mother, and shall be joined unto his wife, and they two shall be one flesh. This is a great mystery: but I speak concerning Christ and the church" (5:30-32).

15. *The enemies of the church are spiritually a part of the kingdom of darkness,* and are not merely jealous human beings. "For we wrestle not against flesh and blood, but against principalities, against powers, against the rulers of the darkness of this world, against spiritual wickedness in high places" (6:12).

THE SPIRITUAL NATURE OF THE CHURCH

The congregation at Ephesus, where St. Paul spent more time than in any other congregation, was instructed about the essentially *spiritual* nature of the congregation. St. Paul had in mind the local Ephesian assembly when he wrote his Epistle, and his readers understood that.

We should not read into his Epistle the universality of the church, a contradiction in terms. The doctrine of a worldwide, visible church as primarily a "universal body" (an impossibility if words have any integrity of meaning) has arisen out of an attempt to justify a "hierarchy" or an overall church structure which governs a number of Christian assembles. A "body" is an *assembled* group, not a party or a movement. To turn the *ekklesia*

Churches of the New Testament Era: Principles

(i.e., "a group called out, called together") into something other than a local assembly is to miss St. Paul's point. The *ekklesia* is a body capable of being assembled. A "scattered assembly" is an impossibility.

A Christian is born again, not into the church but into "the family of God," which is universal and consists of all true believers. Someday these members of the family of God will assemble and thus become a "church." But so far it exists only in prospect. The writer of Hebrews describes it as, "the general assembly and church of the firstborn which are written in heaven" (Hebrews 12:23). When Christ returns, all of the family of God will become *the* church, i.e., the "general assembly."

St. Paul's parting counsel to the church elders of Ephesus revealed his primary concerns for the church. This eyewitness account was written by Luke before the Epistle to the Ephesians was penned by St. Paul from Rome, but it too is important in setting forth church principles.

"For I know this, that after my departing shall grievous wolves enter in among you, not sparing the flock. Also of your own selves shall men arise, speaking perverse things, to draw away disciples after them" (Acts 20:29, 30). The church must beware of dangers from without and within.

The grace of giving was to be paramount in the early church. St. Paul reminded the leaders of his example by saying, "I have coveted no man's silver, or gold, or apparel. Yea, ye yourselves know, that these hands have ministered unto my necessities, and to them that were with me" (20:33, 34).

Paul added that the task of the congregation is to help the weak and to practice a saying of Jesus not recorded in the four Gospels, a rich and noble addition to our knowledge of Him. "I have showed you all things, how that so laboring ye ought to support the weak, and to remember the words of the Lord Jesus, how he said, It is more blessed to give than to receive" (20:35).

The early church had the whole Gospel as its doctrine. St. Paul uses a compelling phrase: "For I have not shunned to declare unto you all the counsel of God" (20:27).

By this he meant both the positive and negative aspects of the truth of God as revealed through Jesus Christ. For example,

Ephesus

"positive thinking" is a biblical truth, but it is only a part of the "whole counsel of God" and comes dangerously near to being a counterfeit Christian message if nothing else is stressed. St. Paul describes the range of his message thus: "And how I kept back nothing that was profitable unto you, but have showed you, and have taught you publicly, and from house to house" (20:20).

The essence of New Testament doctrine was succinctly stated by St. Paul several times. Two notable examples are:

"Testifying both to the Jews, and also to the Greeks, *repentance toward God, and faith toward our Lord Jesus Christ*" (20:21).

"But none of these things move me, neither count I my life dear unto myself, so that I might finish my course with joy, and the ministry, which I have received of the Lord Jesus, *to testify the gospel of the grace of God*" (20:24).

St. Paul describes the task of the minister as follows: "Take heed therefore unto yourselves, and to all the flock, over the which the Holy Ghost hath made you overseers, to feed the church of God, which he hath purchased with his own blood" (20:28).

A Roman tomb on a cliff near Colosse. The plaster still shows traces of first-century decorative painting.

Twelve
COLOSSE

Unlike some of the major cities of the New Testament era, Colosse no longer exists. Many capitals of the ancient world are still major cities. In fact, Jerusalem, Rome, Athens, and Damascus are greater in population today than in the first century. Thessalonika (or Salonika as it is now sometimes called), Joppa, and Antioch are still flourishing centers of commerce.

But Colosse, Caesarea, Ephesus, and Corinth are today only empty sites where important cities once thrived. Colosse alone has the distinction of being still unexcavated, and probably not 100 American Christians have ever explored its mounds and caves. This writer has been there twice, but beheld only wild desolation or farmers' fields.

Yet what an important church was once there. It is still important to us today. Why? First, because Paul wrote the irreplaceable Epistle to the Colossians to that congregation. Then, from Rome along with this Epistle he sent the Epistle to Philemon. The letters to Ephesus and to Laodicea (now lost) were also carried to Colosse by Tychicus and Onesimus; the latter was a voluntarily returned slave, converted through St. Paul's ministry in Rome.

"All my state shall Tychicus declare unto you, who is a beloved brother, and a faithful minister and fellow servant in the Lord: Whom I have sent unto you for the same purpose, that he might know your estate, and comfort your hearts" (Colossians 4:7, 8).

It may be worthwhile to consider the means by which St. Paul's letters have reached us. The very fact that we possess his letter to the church at Colosse and his personal note to Philemon concerning Onesimus is powerful proof that they were preserved, copied, and distributed to other churches by the church

95

at Colosse; that is, they were preserved by the Spirit of God in this way. Would that we had also other letters which St. Paul must have written, but which were not preserved and about which we know nothing.

The church at Colosse, which met in Philemon's house and had Epaphras as its minister-founder, reflected Epaphras himself in its unflagging zeal and energy. St. Paul highly commended him for this. It must have continued to be a flourishing and influential church, although St. Paul never visited it. Its most noted member, Philemon, may have been converted in Ephesus, for St. Paul appears to have known him well enough to lay claim to some great obligation which Philemon owed to him. From his personal reference to this in the letter to Philemon, it appears that there existed an extraordinary bond of Christian love between the two men.

ST. PAUL vs. HERESY IN COLOSSE

We are not dealing primarily with Pauline theology in this book, but with universal principles of the duties, practices, and nature of the churches as revealed in the founding and growth of the apostolic congregations. Those principles which are revealed by the letter of St. Paul to the church at Colosse indicate that heresies had crept in and had to be dealt with by the church. How, in general, did St. Paul encourage them to do this?

1. *By affirming the authority of Jesus Christ as the Head of the church.* For the church, invaded as it had been by false teachings, no *new* doctrine was needed. The truth about Christ was still enough. Christ as Head of the church is the only judge of its doctrines, and He would never approve of the so-called "art of living" in place of the Gospel. "And he is the head of the body, the church: who is the beginning, the firstborn from the dead; that in all things he might have the preeminence" (1:18).

2. *By affirming the necessity of continuing in the faith already revealed.* "To the saints and faithful brethren in Christ which are at Colosse: Grace be unto you, and peace, from God our Father and the Lord Jesus Christ. We give thanks to God and the Father of our Lord Jesus Christ, praying always for you" (1:2, 3).

St. Paul was afraid the winds of false doctrine would blow some members off the path of truth. The Epistle to the Colossians is a message for the church to remain fixed upon the eternal, unchanging Christ; the preexistent Lord; the Christ who dwells in believers by faith; the One whose lordship makes all contrary doctrines an affront to God.

"And ye are complete in him, which is the head of all principality and power" (2:10). How could people improve on Jesus Christ, the Lord of glory? That question needs to be posed to this day!

3. *By affirming that all the knowledge they needed was the knowledge of the mystery of Christ, the fountain of all spiritual wisdom.* "In whom are hid all the treasures of wisdom and knowledge. And this I say, lest any man should beguile you with enticing words" (2:3, 4).

HERESIES IN THE CHURCH AT COLOSSE

GNOSTICISM

The congregation of Colosse had been troubled by the arrival of people who taught various heresies, notably that which later came to be called gnosticism (i.e., being "in the know," possessing special mystical knowledge revealed only to those who were privately instructed). This was "knowledge" which differed in substance from the *truths* of historic and orthodox Christianity, and which supposedly gave its initiates special position and power. Gnostics claimed special knowledge about the nature of Jesus Christ, claiming He was only a man, His divinity being temporarily bestowed and removed before the cross.

Gnosticism was more attractive philosophically than Christian orthodoxy because it comfortably explained away the virgin birth and the divinity of Jesus. It "revealed" how it was possible for the Son of God to die, because it was actually only the man Jesus who died—the "Christ" was above such mortality. Gnosticism was actually a philosophy to be "known" rather than truth to be believed or experienced.

St. Paul fiercely rebutted the Gnostic heresy of "salvation by new knowledge" which was to plague the churches for centuries afterwards. Only Christ, His teachings, and the apostolic doctrines concerning Him were needed, since Christ was and is Lord of all, St. Paul argued.

PHILOSOPHY

St. Paul preached faith in Christ Himself rather than in a mere philosophy. In that sense, he repeated the approach he had used at Athens to the Stoics and Epicureans: "Beware lest any man spoil you through philosophy and vain deceit, after the tradition of men, after the rudiments of the world, and not after Christ" (2:8).

(The reader is urged to reexamine the chapter on Athens and Christianity's confronting the philosophy of the "art of living," as demonstrated on the occasion of St. Paul's visit to Athens.)

LEGALISM

Legalism (keeping the Mosaic law for salvation) was also a problem at Colosse.

"Blotting out the handwriting of ordinances that was against us, which was contrary to us, and took it out of the way, nailing it to his cross; And having spoiled principalities and powers, he made a show of them openly, triumphing over them in it. Let no man therefore judge you in meat, or in drink, or in respect of an holyday, or of the new moon, or of the sabbath days" (2:14-16).

Note that food, drink, feast days, holy days, and even the Sabbath are described as "shadows of things to come; but the body is of Christ" (2:17). Legalism had no place of importance in the early church.

It cannot be overlooked that St. Paul used the Sabbath when he ministered to Jews at their synagogues. However, when he instructed Christians in the faith, he made no attempt to insist they observe the Sabbath. On the contrary, he treated it as of little importance. He described religion consisting of observances of days, customs, and laws, in place of faith in the living Christ, as mere "will-worship"; that is, worshiping according to one's own ego, pleasing one's own sense of self-righteousness. This heresy too has continued to plague the churches ever since St. Paul's day.

Colosse

MYSTICISM

The Colossian church was warned against emphasizing false mysticism and prayers to angels. "Let no man beguile you of your reward in a voluntary humility and worshipping of angels, intruding into those things which he hath not seen, vainly puffed up by his fleshly mind" (2:18).

It is difficult to see how despite this clear teaching by St. Paul, certain churches still observe the worship of angels. Some even call certain angels "saints," though biblically the two terms are totally distinct.

ASCETICISM

"Wherefore if ye be dead with Christ from the rudiments of the world, why, as though living in the world, are ye subject to ordinances, (Touch not; taste not; handle not; Which all are to perish with the using;) after the commandments and doctrines of men?" (2:20-22).

Asceticism, the punishment of the flesh, is a Hindu doctrine, but it ravaged Christianity shortly after the apostolic age. Holiness was considered by the Hindus to belong to the person who most overcame the natural as well as the unnatural desires of the flesh. This aspect of monasticism is not characteristic of the *early* church. By such behavior, the so-called "saints" of the fourth and fifth century, sitting on pillars or walling themselves up in caves, advertised their sanctity, pleased their egos, and satisfied their sense of superiority over "ordinary" Christians. But they would gain no merit with God by asceticism, according to St. Paul.

ST. PAUL ON THE TRUE ART OF LIVING

The "art of Christian living" seen in God's Word is in great contrast with the so-called "art of living" as taught by worldly philosophers. St. Paul dealt at length with this. "Put on therefore, as the elect of God, holy and beloved, bowels of mercies, kindness, humbleness of mind, meekness, longsuffering; Forbearing one another, and forgiving one another, if any man have a quarrel against any: even as Christ forgave you, so also do ye. And above all these things put on charity, which is the bond of perfectness. And let the peace of God rule in your hearts, to the which also ye are called in one body; and be ye thankful" (3:12-15).

The Christian art of living is not ego-centered, but Christ-centered.

ST. PAUL ON CHRISTIAN BEHAVIOR

Different people in the Colossian church were taught ideals of Christian behavior suited to them personally.

Husbands and wives: "Wives, submit yourselves unto your own husbands, as it is fit in the Lord. Husbands, love your wives, and be not bitter against them" (3:18, 19).

Children: "Children, obey your parents in all things: for this is well-pleasing unto the Lord" (3:20).

Fathers: "Fathers, provoke not your children to anger, lest they be discouraged" (3:21).

Servants and masters: "Servants, obey in all things your masters according to the flesh; not with eyeservice, as men-pleasers; but in singleness of heart, fearing God: And whatsoever ye do, do it heartily, as to the Lord, and not unto men; Knowing that of the Lord ye shall receive the reward of the inheritance: for ye serve the Lord Christ. But he that doeth wrong shall receive for the wrong which he hath done: and there is no respect of persons" (3:22-25). "Masters, give unto your servants that which is just and equal; knowing that ye also have a Master in heaven" (4:1).

Daily conversation and behavior by the church members was to be virtuous. "Walk in wisdom toward them that are without, redeeming the time. Let your speech be always with grace, seasoned with salt, that ye may know how ye ought to answer every man" (4:5, 6).

St. Paul left no area of Christian behavior untouched by his counsel. It is a minor point, but still a valid one, that the church member was always considered by St. Paul to be a separated individual, part of the redemptive community, who nevertheless must always show care toward "outsiders" (NASB). In daily speech, as much as in anything, those "inside" the church are to be "wise" toward those "outside." This distinction was lost to members of later state churches where citizenship and "christening" were almost synonymous. (If virtually everyone is "Christian" in a so-called Christian state or country, how can there be a distinction between those "within" and those "without" the church?)

One can see how the apostolic concept of the church as a *separated* congregation of baptized believers was generally abandoned with the rise of state churches. This is not to deny that true Christians can and do exist in state churches, but true New Testament congregations surely have a hard time doing so.

ST. PAUL ON SLAVERY

The Roman Empire was corrupted by human slavery. Slaves frequently made up the majority of the population of Rome and other large cities.

Critics of Christianity have suggested that the institution of slavery was left intact because the early Christians demonstrated little social conscience toward this evil. Perhaps so, but the Epistle to Philemon shows another face to the problem.

It is quite true that St. Paul nowhere directly attacked slavery as an institution. Perhaps this was because the Apostle did not want Christianity to be known primarily as an antislavery crusade, which would have made slavery the issue instead of Christ.

Nevertheless, the seeds of antislavery were certainly sown by St. Paul in his letter to Philemon. His solution was breathtaking: When a person becomes a child of God, he is a brother or sister to all other Christians. Therefore, Onesimus, Philemon's runaway slave, had become a Christian brother to his master. How could the state of slavery then continue?

St. Paul made this abundantly clear. Had all Christians followed the early church in this matter, much anguish would have been prevented. Note carefully what St. Paul wrote to Philemon:

"I beseech thee for my son Onesimus, whom I have begotten

in my bonds: Which in time past was to thee unprofitable, but now profitable to thee and to me: Whom I have sent again: thou therefore receive him, that is, mine own bowels: Whom I would have retained with me, that in thy stead he might have ministered unto me in the bonds of the gospel: But without thy mind would I do nothing; that thy benefit should not be as it were of necessity, but willingly. For perhaps he therefore departed for a season, that thou shouldest receive him for ever; Not now as a servant, but above a servant, a brother beloved, specially to me, but how much more unto thee, both in the flesh, and in the Lord? If thou count me therefore a partner, receive him as myself" (Philemon 10-17).

If all Christians had followed this pattern (and some did), then slavery would have ended long before it did, in Christian-influenced countries anyway.

Have the early churches, which were the creation of the Holy Spirit under the Apostles' ministry, always been followed as divine patterns? In contrast to churches after that period as well as in present times, it is obvious that they have not been. "Will-worship" has never died, even among Christians.

Thirteen
ROME

Rome was the capital of the Roman Empire, which was the greatest historical, political, and cultural influence in the entire Western world for about 800 years. In time, Rome became the foremost "Christian" city of the world.

THE CENTER OF THE EMPIRE

Rome's early history is shrouded in mist, but by 500 B.C. it began to be well-known. The prophet Daniel foresaw that Rome would become a great world power when he wrote his book late in the sixth century B.C. His predictions began to come to pass even before the birth of Jesus.

After the time of Christ, Rome itself lasted as a political center for another 500 years, although it began to fade when Constantine moved the administrative center of the empire to Constantinople (formerly Byzantium) in A.D. 325. Later his successors divided the Roman Empire into eastern and western divisions. Rome was reduced to a provincial city, and at times lay in ruins.

Constantine was mainly responsible for the eventual demise of Rome as the center of imperial Roman power. He was also responsible for the regrettable union of the Christian religion and the state, which eclipsed the primitive, apostolic concept of the church as a *congregation*.

Constantinople did not fall to the Turks until 1453; thus, it could be said to have lasted as the capital of the Roman Empire even longer than Rome itself. Rome held power for 800 years, while the Byzantine civilization endured for over 1,100 years! Yet the Byzantine Empire, in many ways, was at first merely Rome transplanted. So in the broader historical sense, Roman imperial power, though it moved eastward to Constantinople eventually, lasted from 500 B.C. to A.D. 1453, almost 2,000 years. Western history shows no parallel to this amazing longevity of continuous political power. As a religious power, Rome continues to this day.

ST. PAUL AND THE EARLY CHURCHES IN ROME

St. Paul realized the importance of Rome in his strategic planning for world evangelization. He had not visited Rome when he wrote the Epistle to the Roman Christians (A.D. 55); yet he already knew many of the Christians who had moved there intimately. He knew that they needed clear teaching on the Gospel of grace. So he wrote them from Corinth to provide a handbook on how they were to confront the representatives of Judaism and paganism. Both groups were being evangelized by certain Christians, who before St. Paul wrote the Epistle to the Romans had already organized at least four flourishing congregations in Rome, a city of more than a million inhabitants at that time.

St. Paul's task was to establish these churches more firmly in the faith even before he arrived there, which he planned to do as soon as he could. Already, as St. Paul noted, the fame and vigor of the churches of Rome had attracted worldwide attention. St. Paul recognized that in time, the Roman churches would be highly influential in the very rapidly spreading Christian movement. And so it has proved to be.

"First, I thank my God through Jesus Christ for you all, that your faith is spoken of throughout the whole world" (Romans 1:8). "Making request, if by any means now at length I might have a prosperous journey by the will of God to come unto you. For I long to see you, that I may impart unto you some spiritual gift, to the end ye may be established" (1:10, 11). "Now I would not have you ignorant, brethren, that oftentimes I purposed to come unto you, (but was let hitherto,) that I might have some fruit among you also, even as among other Gentiles" (1:13).

TO WHOM WAS THE EPISTLE ADDRESSED?

In the last portion of his book, St. Paul mentions by name a large number of Christians whom he already knew. Among them were both Jews and Gentiles. Some were Christians before he was, and others were kinsmen or beloved friends. Some, undoubtedly, were his converts. The impressive intimacy of his references and greetings to them surely indicate that he had been in correspondence with them regularly, and that they had reported the state of the churches in Rome to him. So he addressed his letter, "To all that be in Rome, beloved of God, called to be saints: Grace to you, and peace, from God our Father and the Lord Jesus Christ" (1:7).

The churches of Rome were composed of at least four groups: Jewish converts; Gentile (ex-pagan) converts; converts from among the Gentiles who were not pagans but moralists who had been attracted to the Jewish community as the vehicle of God's pre-Christian revelation; converts directly from various secular philosophies who did not believe in the gods of pagan worship.

Hence, the congregations of Rome were exceedingly cosmopolitan and mixed.

Their problem was, St. Paul saw, How should the Gospel of Christ be presented to each of the groups which made up the population of Rome? The Jews' objections to Christianity differed from pagans'. "We preach Christ crucified, unto the Jews a stumblingblock, and unto the Greeks foolishness," wrote the Apostle (1 Corinthians 1:23). The Epistle to the Romans was a handbook to present the full Christian message in all its clarity to all of these groups:

"I am debtor both to the Greeks, and to the Barbarians; both to the wise, and to the unwise" (1:14).

"For the wrath of God is revealed from heaven against all ungodliness and unrighteousness of men, who hold the truth in unrighteousness" (1:18).

"But glory, honor, and peace, to every man that worketh good; to the Jew first, and also to the Gentile: For there is no respect of persons with God" (2:10, 11).

We see this even more specifically in the way St. Paul addressed his readers: "Behold, thou art called a Jew, and restest in the law, and makest thy boast of God" (2:17). "For I speak to you Gentiles, inasmuch as I am the apostle of the Gentiles, I magnify mine office" (11:13).

St. Paul stressed the responsibility of the new man in Christ in the church by saying: "And be not conformed to this world: but be ye transformed by the renewing of your mind, that ye may prove what is that good, and acceptable, and perfect will of God. For I say, through the grace given unto me, to every man that is among you, not to think of himself more highly than he ought to think; but to think soberly, according as God hath dealt to every man the measure of faith" (12:2, 3). "Be kindly affectioned one to another with brotherly love; in honor preferring one another" (12:10).

CHURCH PRINCIPLES FROM THE EPISTLE TO THE ROMANS

1. *The need for unity of the members*: "For as we have many members in one body, and all members have not the same office: So we, being many, are one body in Christ, and every one members one of another" (12:4, 5).

2. *The attitudes of the different officers of the church*: "Having then gifts differing according to the grace that is given to us, whether prophecy, let us prophesy according to the proportion of faith; Or ministry, let us wait on our ministering; or he that teacheth, on teaching; Or he that exhorteth, on exhortation: he that giveth, let him do it with simplicity; he that ruleth, with diligence; he that showeth mercy, with cheerfulness" (12:6-8). "Be of the same mind one toward another. Mind not high things, but condescend to men of low estate. Be not wise in your own conceits" (12:16).

3. *Work among the members*: "Be kindly affectioned one to another with brotherly love; in honor preferring one another; Not slothful in business; fervent in spirit; serving the Lord.... Distributing to the necessity of saints; given to hospitality" (12:10, 11, 13).

4. *The relationship of the church to society*: "Recompense to no man evil for evil. Provide things honest in the sight of all men. If it be possible, as much as lieth in you, live peaceably with all men. Dearly beloved, avenge not yourselves, but rather give place unto wrath: for it is written, Vengeance is mine; I will repay, saith the Lord. Therefore if thine enemy hunger, feed

him; if he thirst, give him drink: for in so doing thou shalt heap coals of fire on his head. Be not overcome of evil, but overcome evil with good" (12:17-21).

"Let every soul be subject unto the higher powers. For there is no power but of God: the powers that be are ordained of God. Whosoever therefore resisteth the power, resisteth the ordinance of God: and they that resist shall receive to themselves damnation. For rulers are not a terror to good works, but to the evil. Wilt thou then not be afraid of the power? Do that which is good, and thou shalt have praise of the same: For he is the minister of God to thee for good. But if thou do that which is evil, be afraid; for he beareth not the sword in vain: for he is the minister of God, a revenger to execute wrath upon him that doeth evil. Wherefore ye must needs be subject, not only for wrath, but also for conscience' sake. For, for this cause pay ye tribute also: for they are God's ministers, attending continually upon this very thing. Render therefore to all their dues: tribute to whom tribute is due; custom to whom custom; fear to whom fear; honor to whom honor. Owe no man any thing, but to love one another: for he that loveth another hath fulfilled the law. For this, Thou shalt not commit adultery, Thou shalt not kill, Thou shalt not steal, Thou shalt not bear false witness, Thou shalt not covet; and if there be any other commandment, it is briefly comprehended in this saying, namely, Thou shalt love thy neighbor as thyself" (13:1-9). "Let us walk honestly, as in the day; not in rioting and drunkenness, not in chambering and wantonness, not in strife and envying" (13:13).

5. *Tolerance toward members of the church who differ in minor beliefs*: "Him that is weak in the faith receive ye, but not to doubtful disputations. For one believeth that he may eat all things: another, who is weak, eateth herbs. Let not him that eateth despise him that eateth not; and let not him which eateth not judge him that eateth: for God hath received him. Who art thou that judgest another man's servant? to his own master he standeth or falleth. Yea, he shall be holden up: for God is able to make him stand. One man esteemeth one day above another: another esteemeth every day alike. Let every man be fully persuaded in his own mind. He that regardeth the day, regardeth it unto the Lord; and he that regardeth not the day, to the Lord

he doth not regard it. He that eateth, eateth to the Lord, for he giveth God thanks; and he that eateth not, to the Lord he eateth not, and giveth God thanks" (14:1-6).

"But why dost thou judge thy brother? or why dost thou set at nought thy brother? for we shall all stand before the judgment seat of Christ" (14:10). "Let us not therefore judge one another any more: but judge this rather, that no man put a stumbling-block or an occasion to fall in his brother's way" (14:13). "It is good neither to eat flesh, nor to drink wine, nor any thing whereby thy brother stumbleth, or is offended, or is made weak" (14:21).

6. *Concern for the welfare of fellow Christians*: "We then that are strong ought to bear the infirmities of the weak, and not to please ourselves. Let every one of us please his neighbor for his good to edification" (15:1, 2).

7. *The need for united prayer in the congregations*: "Now I beseech you, brethren, for the Lord Jesus Christ's sake, and for the love of the Spirit, that ye strive together with me in your prayers to God for me" (15:30).

8. *The office of women in the church*: "I commend unto you Phebe our sister, which is a servant [in Greek, lit. "deaconess"] of the church which is at Cenchrea: That ye receive her in the Lord, as becometh saints, and that ye assist her in whatsoever business she hath need of you: for she hath been a succorer of many, and of myself also" (16:1, 2).

9. *The attitude toward those who cause divisions in the church*: "Now I beseech you, brethren, mark them which cause divisions and offenses contrary to the doctrine which ye have learned; and avoid them. For they that are such serve not our Lord Jesus Christ, but their own belly; and by good words and fair speeches deceive the hearts of the simple" (16:17, 18).

All of these attitudes and positions in the churches were first codified in Holy Scripture by St. Paul. They flow naturally out of the life of newborn children of God, and are the logical extension of a new relationship with God and with fellow Christians.

AFTER THE EPISTLE TO THE ROMANS

The Apostle came to Rome, a prisoner, to stand trial before Nero. After two years of teaching all who came to him in his own house, he was acquitted. Later he was arrested again and executed in Rome.

The main doctrine of the Epistle to the Romans, justification by faith, was in time regrettably neglected by the very church of Rome which should have known it best. The fatal fusion of Christianity and the political structure of the pagan state resulted in a change in the concept of the church. There arose "salvation by ceremony," hierarchical orders, the secular power of religion, and a church emphasizing external forms, forms which corrupted pure Christianity and removed from it the simple concept of the church as a congregation in the form envisioned by the Apostles. The "church" became a universal religious organization, governed from the top by prelates and clergy. This concept was unknown to the Apostles.

The Basilica of St. Paul outside the walls of Rome. The first structure here was built by Constantine in A.D. *330. It is the burial place of St. Paul.*

Fourteen
WHAT MEANING HAVE THE EARLY CHURCHES FOR TODAY?

Historically, there have been many attempts to recover the power and persuasive ability of the early churches. They continue to have a mystique and a fascination that historical curiosity alone can't account for. Most of these "restoration" attempts have failed, in whole or in part, for various reasons.

Some Christians have contended that the beliefs, organization, and practices of the early churches were sufficient for the first century, but the world has changed so much that the churches must also change.

Some have gone so far as to set forth the attractive idea that the Holy Spirit is directly behind such change because He is a living influence in God's people, capable of directing change within the churches as circumstances are altered, irrespective of the pattern of the early churches. "New light for changing times" is therefore, according to this argument, perfectly consistent with the nature of the living Holy Spirit, since life always involves change.

Should early Christian doctrine ever be changed? Jude, in the third verse of his Epistle, speaks of "the faith which was once [for all] delivered unto the saints." The phrase "for all" is in the original Greek and emphasizes finality. Changes in doctrine have indeed occurred in Christian history, but the following questions cannot be ignored.

1. Have such changes helped or hurt Christianity?

2. At what point will doctrinal changes so grievously alter Christianity as to remove it from being *true* Christianity?

3. Do we really think successive generations can improve on the doctrines of Jesus Christ and the Spirit-inspired Apostles?

There the argument hangs for each Christian and each churchman to ponder.

111

Churches of the New Testament Era: Principles

If these are the questions to be asked about *doctrine*, are they not also to be posed about the nature and program of the *churches*? Again, we ask:

1. Will changing the concept of the church from the New Testament pattern help or hurt Christianity?

2. If change is permitted, just how much shall occur without utterly transforming the church into something different from that envisioned by the Lord of the church and His Apostles?

3. Can we really *improve* on the church patterns established by Jesus and the Apostles?

It would be banal to reply that we cannot help but change churches from the pattern of the first-century assembly, since our modern culture and technology are manifestly different.

We have pianos and organs, whereas they used harps. We have electric lights; they used oil lamps. We have large buildings, whereas they worshiped in homes, schools, synagogues, and amphitheaters. They evangelized in marketplaces; we have radio and television.

This is to reduce the nature of the church to the mechanical.

One thing is certain. The early Christians readily used *any* place and *any* method available to them so that Christ might be preached. Technology and culture are not the issues today, nor were they then.

The matter is far more complex than that. It is, instead, shall the church be local or universal in concept? Shall power and authority ultimately flow from the congregation, or from a synod or denomination? Who has power over the ministry—the congregation or a hierarchy?

It is clearly evident that the apostolic churches were congregationally governed. Hierarchical power ended, if it ever existed in any sense, with the death of the Apostles. Unless, that is, one insists that the Apostles had power and authority that could be handed intact to successors. A careful examination of the Scriptures seems to this writer to demonstrate conclusively that such a concept was not held in the New Testament era churches.

St. Paul, for example, did not recognize the primacy of St. Peter, as he said in Galatians 1:11-13: "But I certify you, brethren, that the gospel which was preached of me is not after man. For I neither received it of man, neither was I taught it, but by the revelation of Jesus Christ. For ye have heard of my conversation in time past in the Jews' religion, how that beyond measure I persecuted the church of God, and wasted it."

Later on he wrote in Galatians 2:11, "But when Peter was come to Antioch, I withstood him to the face, because he was to be blamed."

Nor did St. Paul hold Christians responsible to him, as he told the Corinthian church: "Not for that we have dominion over your faith, but are helpers of your joy: for by faith ye stand" (2 Corinthians 1:24).

St. Peter referred to St. Paul as "our brother" in his second Epistle and seemed to make no claim for himself, apart from that of being "also an elder": " . . . And account that the long-suffering of our Lord is salvation; even as our beloved brother Paul also according to the wisdom given unto him hath written unto you" (2 Peter 3:15). "The elders which are among you I exhort, who am also an elder, and a witness of the sufferings of Christ, and also a partaker of the glory that shall be revealed: Feed the flock of God which is among you, taking the oversight thereof, not by constraint, but willingly; not for filthy lucre, but of a ready mind; Neither as being lords over God's heritage, but being ensamples to the flock" (2 Peter 5:1-3).

St. James, the brother of Jesus, *not* St. Peter, was the chief elder or bishop of the church in Jerusalem. One of several references to this is found in Acts 15:6, 13, 19, 22:

"And the apostles and elders came together for to consider of this matter. . . . And after they had held their peace, James answered, saying, Men and brethren, hearken unto me: . . . Wherefore my sentence is, that we trouble not them, which from among the Gentiles are turned to God: . . . Then pleased it the apostles and elders, with the whole church, to send chosen men of their own company to Antioch with Paul and Barnabas; namely, Judas surnamed Barsabas, and Silas, chief men among the brethren."

SUMMARY

This book is not intended to be an anti-Catholic polemic. Much good has come from, and been preserved by, both the

Churches of the New Testament Era: Principles

Roman and Greek churches. However, there is a danger in the tendency of substituting a power structure which seems to grow naturally in many quarters, unless there is a regular and firm reversal which revives the organizational principles of the New Testament era churches.

We *hope* that *we* may be guided by the Holy Spirit today in all church matters, but we *know* the Apostles had the mind of the Spirit and were empowered and commissioned by Him in the way that *they* organized churches!

We can testify from a study of the differences in the early churches that the Spirit is flexible, dealing as He must with people of differing cultures. Flexibility is one thing, but disagreement with the Spirit-inspired-Apostles is something else.

Building and administering effective congregations today is not easy. But we do have a clear guide in the New Testament, telling us how Jesus and His instructed followers did it. By following their principles, we too can build strong congregations.

Part Two

NEW TESTAMENT CHURCHES TODAY: PRACTICAL APPLICATION

Introduction
THE NEW TESTAMENT CHURCH TODAY

The preceding careful study of certain churches in the New Testament era has not revealed any one which incorporated all the aspects which were generally descriptive of all of them. They each bore a fairly close resemblance to the norm, but it is evident that there was no such thing as the ideal church.

We should not be surprised at this, since the raw material of the church in any age is human nature (regenerated but human) with all of its frailties.

Nevertheless, this study is only a review of history unless it is translated into a clearly understandable pattern which can be followed by churches today.

This section deals with a description of New Testament patterns for the church as a "spiritual community." This is a concept which can apply the primitive patterns for the church to contemporary congregations.

117

The author at the Mamertine Prison, Rome—undoubtedly the place where St. Paul and St. Peter were held by Nero.

Fifteen
CAN THE CHURCH SURVIVE THE TWENTIETH CENTURY?

In 1933, at the Chicago World Fair, one striking exhibit was called "The City of Tomorrow." The most imaginative architectural designers in the nation had pooled their insights, skill, and knowledge to produce a wonder city in miniature. Six-lane highways, four and five deep, crossing over and under each other, kept traffic flowing. Airports were on top of gigantic skyscrapers. Moving sidewalks carried people from store to store. Functional structures of aluminum, glass, and synthetic materials loomed above the city.

The first summer of exhibition was almost half finished when a puzzled spectator approached the display manager with the query, "Where are the churches?" The manager was quiet. Then, somewhat embarrassed, he said, "Sir, we did not think there would be any need for churches in the city of the future!"

The burning issue facing farsighted Christians today is, "Can the church indeed survive the twentieth century?"

World history has turned a corner in recent days. Almost imperceptibly we have entered a new age based upon scientific technology. Man has traveled further back into inner space than can be imagined, until he has laid hands on the tiniest particles of the atom. Then within a few years he took the first steps toward traveling in outer space at speeds and distances that defy understanding. What have these two journeys into inner and outer space taught us? Most of all, that we are living in a new age and all things must now be reexamined and tested. Even the church is not exempt from this rigorous scrutiny.

Christians want to know, "How will the church fit into the new space age?" Can it remain the same? Must it change its methods, or its message? Will it flourish or fail? Is it possible the world could get along without the church? Is it likely the

New Testament Churches Today: Practical Application

City of Tomorrow will be built with no room or planning for churches, because the churches will have no vital role in the coming age? These are the great questions of our times for Christians to ponder.

All of the world's ills can be directly traced to the fact that there are not enough *real* Christians to go around. There never have been and never will be. But it is the business of the churches of Jesus Christ to produce and encourage real Christians. There is no other institution which can provide them. Either the church must do this, its primary job, or fail. Yet Dr. Roy Burkhart quotes Reinhold Niebuhr as saying:

> The church as it now stands is increasingly irrelevant
> to the average man and must suffer a rebirth or face
> the inevitable consequence of being unable to survive
> in its present form.

As badly as the world needs the church, there are unmistakable signs of a possible passing away of the church as we know it.

Even Jesus asked His disciples: "When the Son of man cometh, *shall* he find Faith on the earth?" This was not a statement or prophecy, but a question, for the answer is up to *us*.

Billy Graham addressed the Methodist Assembly at Lake Junaluska, N.C., with the statement:

> If the church does not meet its responsibilities in this
> generation, it may go into eclipse!

Speaking at the First Presbyterian Church of Columbia, South Carolina, Dr. Norman G. Dunning of Hull University, England, made this observation:

> Dull, unexciting religion has emptied the churches of
> Europe since the beginning of this century, and it will
> do it for you in America before the century closes
> unless you are very careful. I have watched your
> country for a whole generation. I can see in the
> church life of America precisely the same symptoms

120

Can the Church Survive the Twentieth Century?

> I could see in the church life of my own country when
> I began my ministry (in 1924). . . . We had better heed
> the voice of God.

Dr. Leslie Weatherhead's warning is pertinent:

> The Kingdom of Christ on earth may be coming
> either through, or in spite of, the Church as it is now
> organized. And if the latter, then what is now called
> the Church will cease to be the Church. For that
> eternal reality is not a man-made thing of form or
> convention. It exists only where the Spirit of Jesus
> is alive, active, and communicable.

If Christ shall tarry, I believe the church will survive. But I
also believe it may have to change its methods if it is to remain
vital in this changing age. The message we preach is eternal,
but the methods by which it is presented are temporal and must
always be adaptable to human needs. Leslie Weatherhead said
as much:

> I should be glad to think that at last we had enough
> courage to change our methods. Surely, the Church
> of the future will do so. No doctor in London is using
> only the methods which were used fifty years ago.
> Are we quite sure that religion can best be "put over"
> by two services each Sunday, always proceeding in
> the same way—hymn, prayer, hymn, lesson, etc.?

As a Christian, I am concerned about the survival of the
church. I would like to know there will be a future church and
try to help my congregation be that church today! Ibsen's words
deserve serious consideration:

> I hold, that man is right who is most closely in
> league with the future!

The churches cannot afford to guess wrong about the future.

121

New Testament Churches Today: Practical Application

They must study the trends of our times, or the future will find us fighting a new war with the obsolete weapons of the last war.

There is no predestined certainty that the church will survive the next half century! Those who quote "The gates of hell shall not prevail against it" as the guarantee that the church cannot fail, are missing the illustration. Gates belong to a city, a fortress, a castle. As long as the church *is on the march*, taking the initiative, storming the gates even of Hell itself, nothing can stand before it. The gates of Hell will neither stand nor prevail, but will fall before the onslaught.

But the church that stays in camp will never break down the doors of the citadel of sin. God says that such churches cannot become victorious, and indeed are doomed to death. To the church at Sardis, Jesus said: "Thou hast a name that thou livest, and art dead" (Revelation 3:10).

So *churches can die*. In China there was once a flourishing Christian movement, begun in the Middle Ages. But when the first missionaries from America went there 150 years ago, they found no Chinese Christians at all. The Christian faith, once hardy, had died completely.

In Philadelphia, in Asia, a church which once rejoiced in the promise of Christ ("I have set before thee an open door," Revelation 3:8) now is dead. When I visited there, I found the city itself completely Moslem. The white minaret of a new Mohammedan mosque was framed by the ruined buttresses of the ancient Christian church, long since abandoned.

Don't say it can't happen here in America. It is happening before our eyes in England. Once it was the most Christian of nations, with the greatest pulpits and preachers in the world. Now dry rot has set in, and less than 5 percent of the British people are said to attend the average Sunday worship services of the church. The paganizing of England is one of the sad facts of our time. Russia too has gone down the path of spiritual declension. In Jerusalem and the Middle East, the home of the Christian faith, there is so little Gospel being preached that few localities seem as utterly, and literally, God-forsaken. In many other places in the world, the church has died. It could happen here. Look at the evidence around you.

Can the Church Survive the Twentieth Century?

Even a casual observer cannot help but see that Christianity is in for the greatest and fiercest competition it has ever known in any one era since the first century. It would seem that this competition is to come from four main sources.

1. *Communism*. This dread Antichrist, this false religion, this miserable counterfeit which promises freedom and sells nations into slavery, is our deadly enemy. Historians call it "a perversion of Christianity." Perhaps it is, and all the more to be feared. Sixty years ago its followers were counted in hundreds. Today one third of the human race wears its chains. Christianity and Communism are waging, and must wage, a war of extermination. Ultimately only one can survive.

2. *Pleasure*. From earliest times the Bible has warned: "But she that liveth in pleasure is dead while she liveth" (1 Timothy 5:6). Never has pleasure been more available to all people than it is today, and we have only seen the beginning. Automobiles, pleasures in themselves, now whisk us to sites of pleasure in minutes, over distances it took our fathers days to travel. What is this doing, and what will it do, to church attendance in times to come? Television will increasingly dominate our lives and crowd out the evening services at the church. Country homes and sporting recreations such as boating take us away from the house of God as Sunday becomes a holiday instead of a holy day. Labor leaders propose a four-day work week. If it should come in the next twenty-five years (and what is to prevent it?), the "long weekend" will fill our highways and airplanes, and empty our churches!

God is not the enemy of legitimate pleasures, for He created us with the capacity to enjoy them. But when pleasure becomes our god, it becomes an enemy of the true God, who for our sakes is a jealous God and who will have none else beside Him.

3. *False faiths*. The trend of our times is toward an amalgamated religion that honors all religions alike (so the historian Toynbee predicts). Our interfaith "brotherhood" movements encourage it. Our desire for easy religion demands it. The rise of modern cults confirms it. Let us remember that every conversion to false faiths, and the continued success and growth of ancient heresies and paganisms is not only a gain for them, but a loss to true Christianity.

123

4. *Materialism.* We need to reevaluate this monster, for it grows so subtly that its very appeal to one's love for ease and convenience lulls us into fatal intolerance. Even our faith becomes materialistic if we are not careful. When man tries to use God, or "try" prayer, or "believe" for the sake of his own selfish ends, then Christianity has become "non-Christianity." The desire for money will lead us away from worship, so we have more time to labor. The compelling need for possessions and comforts wins us away from tithing, from sacrifice, from the cross, and to convenient religion. Convenient Christianity has lost its "first love" and because it is neither hot nor cold, God may spew it out of His mouth!

This is, then, an incomplete but indicative list of the very real competition Christianity faces. Early Christians recognized the dangers. Paul complained: "Demas hath forsaken me, having *loved this present world*" (2 Timothy 4:10).

Before this he predicted: "For men shall be lovers of their own selves, covetous, boasters, proud, blasphemers, disobedient to parents, unthankful, unholy, without natural affection, trucebreakers, false accusers, incontinent, fierce, despisers of those that are good, traitors, heady, high-minded, lovers of pleasures more than lovers of God" (2 Timothy 3:2-4).

It would seem these days are now with us. For the first time in history we are faced with the technology of pleasure, the atheistic theory of government, the pressure of materialism from innumerable advertisements. The churches are in for rough days! Can they survive or will they be reduced to impotence? Does it seem silly to ask this when at present it is so obvious that the churches were never more crowded and prosperous?

There is serious question as to whether the recent religious revival in America is superficial or likely to last. Crowded churches do not necessarily indicate a revival of true faith, any more than crowded highways mean people are becoming better drivers. Unless the people become enlisted in total Christianity, the well-traveled highways of religion may only accelerate our failure. My feeling is that the tide will eventually go out again and not return so full in our time.

"Crowded churches," said one reporter, "merely mean that

124

Can the Church Survive the Twentieth Century?

the people are shopping, and if they don't find something to buy, in my judgment, one of these days there is going to be the greatest falling away from the church that we have seen in many a year!"

I believe that Christianity is certainly in danger of losing its momentum, and may actually have to battle even to survive. The time for this may be nearer than we have realized.

The church cannot grow if it ceases to take the offensive and to evangelize each new generation and witness to pagan nations of the world (including our own) in this present generation.

The church will fail unless it discovers a way to again become *revolutionary* in its appeal to people and their needs.

The Augsburg Uniform Lessons have hopefully suggested that 500 years from now historians may say about our times:

> The twentieth century was one of the most upsetting periods in history. Drastic changes in the pattern of living were made due to dramatic scientific and technological discoveries. More disastrous, the social patterns of the whole world were ruthlessly torn apart in the struggle for world dominance. Only *the emergence of a new prophetic movement within the Christian church saved the human race from self-destruction and helped set the pattern for the culture of this* year, 2500 A.D.

It is now the purpose of this study to suggest what that "prophetic movement in Christianity" may and can be. It is *nothing more or less than a rediscovery of the true nature and purpose of the local congregation, called in the New Testament "the church."*

In his timely study of the church, H. Richard Niebuhr says:

> The definition of the church—even the awareness of its actuality—constitutes one of the main concerns of modern theology. Without a definition of Church it is impossible to define adequately the work of the ministry for which the school is to prepare its students.[1]

[1] *The Purpose of the Church and Its Ministry* (New York: Harper and Row, 1977), n.p.

New Testament Churches Today: Practical Application

It is to be feared, however, that with the attempt to lay emphasis upon some other aspect of the church than that of the local congregation, we have overlooked the obvious truth that in ninety out of one hundred times in the Bible, the *ekklesia* or "church" spoken of is a certain specific congregation or "assembly."

In our zeal for a denominational "church" or an ecumenical "church," we have overlooked the "assembly." I believe a rediscovery of God's true purpose and program for the "assembly" will bring about the condition for dynamic revival in Christianity in the truest sense of that much misused word.

As evangelical Christians we find the Scriptures (and before them, the living Word, Christ), the authoritative source of our doctrines, church government, ideas of a "called" ministry, church policies, and the definition of the purpose of the church in the mind of Christ.

The New Testament gives the patterns we believe we should follow in all matters of faith, doctrine, and practice.

But there yet remains one step more for us to take if we are, as a people, to be truly "New Testament" churches. *We must adopt the New Testament program for the church*!

Evangelical Christians have been rather consistent in adopting the New Testament doctrines, organization, church policy, and discipline for their churches. But only to a limited degree have we gone all the way back to the conscious restoration of the New Testament *program* in our churches today.

There are three reasons why we should do this.

1. In view of the terrific competition that lies ahead, threatening the very life of the churches, no less than the New Testament program will do!

2. Pragmatic tests have proven that the New Testament pattern of church program works! In all ages, in all lands, present and future, it will work.

3. Jesus gave us the pattern of His divine program by the administration of divinely called "pastors" in Jerusalem whom He called Apostles. We cannot improve on His doctrines; we cannot improve upon His program!

Christianity cannot survive if the churches do not survive. Yet many Christian leaders work in complete indifference to the assembly, almost as if it did not exist or did not matter. Other leaders have no awareness of the importance of the assembly in the plan of God and therefore stunt its growth, or at best never realize the potential that is inherent in the assembly.

We shall find the term "spiritual or redemptive community" as the best description of the New Testament church.

Over the door of this cathedral in Athens are the words, "In honor of Dionysius the Areopagite, St. Paul's first convert in Athens."

Sixteen
WHICH CHURCH IS THE TRUE CHURCH?

This is not an attempt to prove that any particular denomination is "true," while maintaining that all others are "false." The question of truth and falsity is to be decided not only by the position certain denominations take on church doctrines. One cannot choose beliefs, sincerely held by others, and use them as a sort of measuring stick marking the only boundary between the true church and the false.

If this were done, and it *is* being done too often, there would be many churches which might be quite orthodox in doctrine but are in no sense true churches. There would probably be others, which by the standards of orthodoxy would be heretical on some points, yet which are *better than their doctrines* and which meet many of the requirements of a true church.

What then do we mean by *"true church?" We mean the church as conceived in the mind of Christ and as established by Him in Jerusalem*. We can be sure the Apostles knew precisely what Jesus meant for the church to be and to do. Our urgent task is to discover this afresh. It is no small task because we have accumulated so much tradition, so much religious prejudice, that a formidable job of clearing these away awaits us. There are at least ten definitions of the word "church" itself. The man on the street, and even the member in the pew, has neither a clear concept of the word, nor even an awareness that it is important to understand it.

This study is no mere academic debate over the meaning of words of interest only to theologians. The very existence of Christianity is at stake, faced as it is by the rise of Antichrist. The church cannot go on the offensive unless it knows what it is and has a clear concept of why it has the right to survive and prevail!

New Testament Churches Today: Practical Application

No one can seriously contend that Christianity as a whole is on the march. Segments of it are. But Christianity has generally lost a clear picture of the relationship of itself to the church. We should realize that the church is not always identical with Christianity. It is precisely the difference between them which needs to be understood, so the church can play its part in the preservation of Christianity.

We must begin with fundamentals. The word *church* is an Anglo-Saxon word which we use as the equivalent of the Greek word *ekklesia*. This word, *ekklesia*, was used to describe the assembly or congregation of citizens in the ancient cities of Greece, meeting to decide affairs of public interest. It was somewhat like a town meeting of responsible citizens.

Now note that the *ekklesia* was only in existence *when it was meeting in a body*. When it dispersed, it ceased to exist until the next time it met.

An *ekklesia* had a membership, but it did not function except when gathered. This is evident from the root meaning of the word: *ek*=out; *klesia*=to call. The idea was that this was a group of people who were called out of their homes and businesses to confer as a body. The body was the *ekklesia*.

The emphasis was not on what they had been called out *from*, but what they had been called out *to*. Thus the correct translation of *ekklesia* is "assembly."

When Jesus used the word *ekklesia* to describe a new body He was founding to carry on His work, He plainly meant that His *ekklesia* was to be His *assembly*. Today the word church (originally "assembly") has been perverted to mean so many other things that we have missed in many ways Christ's intention for this body or assembly; we no longer seem to care what He intended. We have instead read into it what we think it ought to mean.

For example, when a denomination calls itself a "church," it is distorting the word. It cannot fully assemble, so it is not an "assembly" or *ekklesia*. A well-known radio preacher refers to his listeners as "his church." His listeners cannot assemble, they cannot vote, they cannot have fellowship, they cannot function as a body. They may be a part of a Christian move-

Which Church Is the True Church?

ment, but *they are not a church* by any stretch of the imagination —if the Bible is to be our source of definition.

We must get back to the original concept of the church as Christ taught it and the Apostles organized it. But even if we do recognize that only the assembly of Christians is the original "church," we still must discover the elements which make an assembly a *true* church.

This is not to say that the assembly is the only form which Christianity should take. There must also be evangelistic organizations, missionary fellowships, denominations, Christian radio programs, and so on. But these things are not the church. Blessed by God and essential as they are, the church is the central organization in the mind of God. It is the only organization Jesus founded.

We still have not completely defined what a true church is. Merely assembling does not make a church true! It is the starting point but only that. The entire New Testament at great length spells out what the true church is and does. It takes this entire study to cover the scope of this subject.

Let us rid our minds of all traditional ideas and definitions of the *ekklesia* for at least the time required for this study and get back to the simple, original intention which Jesus had for it. Let us see how the assembly which consciously does His will can prevail. The gates of Hell are under attack by the true church as it takes the offensive. But such an offensive is not likely unless we discover the true church and liberate it from the misunderstandings, weaknesses, perversions, and downgrading it is now suffering.

The assembly or church is not just a clever idea or a modern method for the promotion of Christianity. It is the result of a divine directive. It is the body or assembly of Christ to carry out His intentions. If the church or assembly were to die, it is certain Christianity could not long survive.

Very few externals are essential for the establishment of a true church—only people committed to Christ and His purposes. True churches can be found in homes, in stores, in church buildings, or in cathedrals.

Old church organizations may have begun as true churches,

but degenerated so that they are no longer true churches but hollow forms. On the other hand, true churches have come to life again in all sorts of existing church organizations which have ceased to be churches in the true sense.

There are no denominational limits to the establishment of true churches. There are true churches everywhere, in all Christian denominations. On the other hand there are church organizations which would be astonished to learn, by a New Testament definition, that *church* in its true sense is totally missing among them, despite a learned clergy, gowned choirs, and Gothic buildings.

THE ACID TEST

There is one characteristic of the true church which should be emphasized at the outset. It is this characteristic which clearly marks one difference between a true and false church—and it is not merely a doctrinal difference. It is simply that a true church leads its people to trust in *Christ Himself* for salvation, rather than in a *church system*.

If a Roman Catholic trusts that he shall be received by God because he belongs to the Roman Catholic system, he is undone. If he is as an individual believer trusting in the saving grace of Christ Himself, and looks to his church as a source of fellowship or work, he is saved.

If a Baptist believes he shall be saved merely because he is a Baptist, orthodox and correct, he is lost. If he depends entirely upon the living Christ, he is saved. If a Methodist trusts his identification with his denomination with its traditions and organizations to save him, he is deluded and lost. If he trusts in the merits of Christ, he is saved.

If a Jehovah's Witness expects salvation because of his system of biblical interpretation, his willingness to witness, his identification with an active army of religious zealots, he is lost, no matter how religious he may be. But if he trusts in the person of the living Christ, the only begotten Son of God, he can be saved in spite of his other heretical doctrines. These examples will suffice.

Which Church Is the True Church?

It must be apparent that while no person can be saved *because* of his doctrines, some must be saved in *spite* of them. But the important difference between the false and the true is whether men are led to trust in Christ, or instead in a religious system for their forgiveness and salvation.

There are hundreds of denominations, scores of heresies, thousands of doctrinal peculiarities in the whole of Christianity. But in the final analysis there is but one basic heresy! That is to trust in a system of religion, instead of in Christ.

I once corresponded with the great C. S. Lewis. I asked him, "What degree of heresy may a denomination in Christianity allow before it crosses the line where it no longer has the power to save?" He replied, "Christianity does not save. Christ alone saves." It was a rebuke well-deserved. I had always believed that Christ alone could redeem, but I was concerned about what degree of heresy churches could endure without ceasing to be truly Christian. (This was what I *meant*, despite the awkward way I asked my question!) Nevertheless Mr. Lewis's observation was more profound than my question.

I am quite certain that there is, ultimately, only one heresy, and that is leading men to primarily trust in a religious system (whether that system be your system or mine!) instead of in Christ.

At the same time, you do not define a Christian by his doctrines alone. Christianity is more than doctrine. It is the loving community of God's people gathered to learn, to witness, and to experience the power of God.

CHRISTIANITY—POWER OR PRISON?

It is an interesting exercise to interview an average church member as to why he is a professing Christian, and what he expects Christ to do for him. It has been my experience that all *good* Christians (that is, happy, victorious, responsible Christians) look upon Christianity as *power*. The unhappy, duty-driven, fearful, rebellious Christians who are afraid not to be Christians look upon their Christianity as a *prison*.

Perhaps as young people they were given the subconscious impression that Christianity was only a system of commandments, a series of "thou shalt nots," confining them and regimenting all the "fun" out of life. There is no more grim heresy than this. True, on occasion Christianity demands the utmost sacrifice. It insists that the moral laws of God are binding.

But the true church will attempt to bring the *power* of God into the life of man. The nature of God's power is not to bind but to liberate. "Love Christ, surrender to Him—then do as you please!" is not the foolish liberalism it may seem. To surrender to Christ *is* to obey the moral law—but not legalistically. That is why Jesus could say that all the commandments are fulfilled by loving God and loving man.

We should help young people to see that Christianity, when well understood, is a glorious, powerful, liberating force! No one is ashamed of power—only weakness. I fear we have generally failed at this point.

What then is the relationship of the moral laws and commandments of the Bible to Christianity? For one thing, they are like the ABC's. To spell or write, one has to learn the alphabet. This is a "must," but not a confining "must." It is liberating. A gifted writer does not consider the discipline of the ABC's as a fetter. He must indeed enter his profession through the doors of the alphabet and the laws of grammar, but once mastered *they set him free* to exercise his talents without restraint. So with the moral laws of God. They are not confining but liberating. James called them "the perfect law of liberty" (1:25).

When we obey the laws of God we are freed from the terror of the rebel, the fear of the unknown, the aimlessness of the wanderer, the purposelessness of the worldling. We are no longer enslaved to sin and habits of evil—but are empowered by the very power of God Himself.

The purpose of the true church is to set people free, to display the Christian faith as a source of great power. All the activities of the true church should be aimed at this purpose. Phariseeism may confine within its restrictive system, but the true church releases every power and breaks every chain which would enslave us. For this reason we must always emphasize the liberating and empowering nature of the laws of God, lest only the rigidity of the high moral purpose of the Gospel take precedence in the minds of the uninstructed.

Seventeen
THE CHURCH—THE LAST REFUGE OF PERSONALIZATION

Some educational programs in our school systems insist on conformity and cooperation within one's peer group. Thus the child lives in an environment of conformity which grows increasingly dominant as he finishes high school. By the time the pupil becomes mature, the pattern of conformity is well ingrained.

Society in its present overorganization tends to squeeze individualism out in favor of the adjusted group. In business a person may become "the organization man." In government service he often becomes a listless bureaucrat. The giant unions represent anonymous workers, but not craftsmen. The public is encouraged to think favorably of mass activities, mass entertainment, and mass sports based upon observation, not participation. The television audience is a mass audience, and the effect of the "one-eyed monster in the living room" is to lower the standards of taste and sentiment. Tract housing developments are spreading their dreary patterns of conformity, like some cheap clothing which is bright at first but whose color soon fades.

The net effect is to accelerate the thrust toward the collectivized anthill wherein a person is valued for his contribution to society rather than for his inherent worth as a person. The rarity of the owner-farm, the absence of the old-style village, the proliferation of the megalopolis—all this has made the problem of depersonalization acute, distressing, and immediate.

Any pastor or church which is unaware of this factor of depersonalization is simply not taking notice of a trend which has already invaded and killed Protestantism as a vital factor in many industrial cities of the East, except in the suburbs. This is probably the cause of the decline of Christianity in the large industrial towns of England. It is fashionable to blame the influx of Catholic immigration in the factory towns of the Eastern seaboard for the Protestant church losses. But we have overlooked the fact that the Protestant church should be a bastion of personalization. When it is not, it becomes weak and loses by default.

The whole question can thus be asked: In an age in which depersonalization is taking individuality from people as a result of the sociological forces which we have already listed, and when many churches are slowly dying, *what should the church's strategy be*?

Obviously, if Christianity is to remain vital and keep up in growth with the population explosion, the church must change its program and, among other things, become a strong citadel of personalization. If people can turn nowhere else for refuge, let them turn to the church. There, each person is of intrinsic value to God. The church touches life, or should, at the moments which are most truly personal: birth, marriage, grief, loss, friendship, sickness, salvation, and death. Can any other institution make this claim?

But if this concept of the church is to be strengthened to deal adequately with the burgeoning force of depersonalization, it must change its program. Most of all, it must rediscover the image it should have of itself. It must see its task as primarily relating the individual to God, and in the process strengthening each Christian's self-awareness as a child of God, a child who gains identity and self-fulfillment from knowing who he is (and this comes by knowing whom and what he belongs to).

We get identity by *belonging*; not to ourselves, but to great causes, to institutions, to persons beyond ourselves. The church offers this sense of identity more keenly and more vitally than other institutions, for the very reason that God is the Supreme Being to whom we can belong and His Kingdom the supreme cause to which we can give our allegiance.

This spells out specifically and precisely the right program for the church. If this program is successful, it will result in the church becoming a refuge against depersonalization. It will also make the church a center of resistance against socialism, a secularization of the true Kingdom of God; it is a cruel, decep-

The Church—the Last Refuge of Personalization

tive counterfeit which only succeeds in imprisoning people permanently in the vast facelessness of the collectivized state.

Socialism, despite its popularity among many of the "liberal" clergy, is not the "social application of Christianity," as the socialists would have us believe. Instead, it is a coercive measure intended to deprive those who work of the right to own and control what they have earned (i.e., property rights) in the name of a mistaken idealism that only leads to national poverty.

The clergy should battle for the preservation of property rights and condemn as evil, taxation whose purpose is not protection but social control. Property rights *are* human rights—the most basic rights of all, the rights upon which all other rights depend. Take away property rights and civil rights become paper privileges.

With property rights under massive attack in the U.S.A., as well as in other parts of the world, the churches, as the last stronghold of personalization, should rise to lead the fight against socialism. But this is not the case. The clergy seem instead to have been brainwashed by socialistic propaganda to the point where legalized socialistic plunder has been accepted as "Christian." Those who defend "free enterprise under God" are smeared as defenders of "decadent, self-interest groups and greedy capitalists or profiteers." This charge is false.

The layman looks to the church for defense against socialism, since traditional "free enterprise under God" seems to have few friends in government or among the cultural leaders of such professional groups as education, law, and politics. Church members are beginning to be disillusioned with the politically liberal clergy. If the church cannot see the moral issues at stake in the fearful rise of government power, greed, and interference, then where shall laymen turn to hear the prophetic voice? This is one cause of the decline of respect for the churches and the clergy, and this decline of confidence is accelerating. Churches are going to lose members and support over this issue!

"Social justice" has become a smoke screen to cover the socialist plotters. Few, if any, socialists have a New Testament faith, which among other things commands a respect for private property and the responsibility of each to work or not to eat. (Even in the case of the sharing of wealth which was temporarily practiced in the Jerusalem church, the Apostle Peter carefully pointed out that such sharing was voluntary and that property was to be given only if the donor chose to give it. You will search the New Testament in vain for approval of socialism of any kind.)

There is no doubt that the failure of the clergy to take the offensive against the communist menace and the socialist peril is the cause of much church member disaffection. The old truism that the church is intrinsically the best defense against communism is sheer nonsense if the church fosters socialism! The church should arouse a moral crusade against all forms of statism, including socialism, democratic or otherwise. America's sickening unwillingness to take the political and spiritual offensive in the cold war is directly traceable to the utopian socialistic hope that communism can be "contained" and that it will eventually moderate its blood-lust to conquer the earth. Whenever the church becomes the abettor of this appeasement, it hastens the certainty of war, for it encourages national weakness and enemy aggression.

Many laymen know this full well and cannot understand why an educated clergy does not know it too. Loyalty to Jesus Christ demands, in the name of the freedom which He gives, that the Christian churches call the nation to strengthen its policy to destroy communism and socialism by a spiritual and political offensive! Anything less will most assuredly result in the death of freedom and the destruction of the churches. In communist lands the churches are almost dead, and in socialist countries they are fearfully weak. The decline of the churches will be in direct proportion to the rise of socialism in America too!

Eighteen

THE CHURCH AS A SPIRITUAL COMMUNITY

Our picture or concept of the church has a tremendous influence on our management and operation of the church. If we see it as a house of worship, we will dwell on the practices of worship. If we see it as merely an audience, we will overemphasize preaching and perhaps neglect other aspects of the program. If we see the church merely as a social club within a moral environment, we may overstress fellowship for its own sake.

When a church is mainly a "holy band" (this incorrect view is mindful of the old hymn, "Come then and join this holy band and on to glory go"), then it will withdraw within its pietistic shell and become exclusive. When a church sees itself as primarily an evangelistic center, it may find difficulty in educating and developing its people in any well-rounded way.

Surely it is obvious that the *whole* church demands a *whole* program. The true church attempts to see itself as a family, or eventually a community, of believers with as many diverse activities as a civic community. It will include the things which are mentioned above, but will go far beyond them.

Our concern should be to make the church a center of life—relating it to all the needs of all the people. There are few areas of life that cannot center around the church. However, to be a life-centered church the very first requisite is a pastor who sees clearly the larger concept of the church as a spiritual community. He must believe that this was Christ's concept for His church and must throw himself into it—mind, body, time, and heart! He cannot "play church," nor will he be able to engage in too many civic activities, hobbies, or sports. The church as community must be his passion, and the welfare of his people his prime concern. In the spiritual community concept of the church, he does not reign as king, but serves as shepherd.

139

He brings into great responsibility other ministers as rapidly as their activity pays their way. (Each new minister added to the multiple ministry or departmentalized-ministry-concept should "pay" his own way in terms of new people enlisted—only this is justification for additional staff members. There is no real practical limit to the number of ministers, provided each personally enlists enough new members to increase the offerings to cover the additional salary and operational costs. A minister of music with many choirs of all ages can, for example, so materially increase the number of people attending that the increase in collections can pay for his work.) We should not overlook the possibility of nonsalaried ministers either.

But behind all this is the concept that the senior pastor is the coach of the team! No man by himself can carry the responsibility for the spiritual community. This is one of the big reasons why we have so many churches which have more limited concepts of the church. Pastors fall back from the work or time requirements of the spiritual community—never understanding that the multiple ministry, paid or unpaid, is an absolute requirement for the true church.

This is also an indictment of those ministers who refuse to sponsor a spiritual community because they cannot allow other ministers besides themselves to hold authority. An insecure ego that does not dare to delegate authority means not only a sick man, but a sick church. A pulpit is not a throne but a place for one of the members to stand, as he fulfills his calling in the role of one of the flock who has been called upon by God to teach the flock.

Spiritual community-type churches are happy churches. Unlike the one-man ministry, the multiple ministry gives to many the same opportunity of fulfillment which one minister alone enjoys in many churches. Any minister, if he could only realize it, is never more secure than when he delegates, to many members and other ministers, the manifold tasks of the spiritual community. He is thus left free to exercise his greatest gifts instead of having to be "in" on every last activity of the church.

It is at this point the senior minister makes a decision as to whether the church will be a citadel of personalization or join the other social forces in exerting a depersonalizing influence

The Church as a Spiritual Community

upon his members. If only a few people share real responsibility, the rest are only spectators and thus are easily distracted when another competing spectacle comes along.

You can see how this works quite easily. Give out hundreds of tasks to be done regularly in the church (in the choirs, Sunday school, committees, and similar jobs) and the persons performing these tasks will *be* there—rain or shine. Other attractions may tempt, but they will not easily distract.

People gather in groups, but they *think* as individuals. When they no longer count as individuals, they soon lose interest. Only the spiritual community can put enough people to work in enough varied tasks as to utilize every talent and every person. Churches which do not stress the creation of jobs for members will soon have unhappy members. People want to be used by the church. Thus they feel they are advancing the Kingdom of God, and in so doing they find meaning and purpose for their lives in a way far beyond the routine duties of life.

But it is not enough to create jobs. These jobs must be tied in with the theory of the redemptive community. The strongest motive for church attendance will always be the joy that comes from helping to redeem others. That all of us want to be redeemed ourselves, in so many ways, is obvious. But an even stronger desire is to make our own life count by working for the redemption of others. Thus, in a subtle way perhaps, we find redemption by redeeming. Many a father has gotten right with God that he might set a Christian example to his son!

But we must beware lest we set too narrow boundaries around what we mean by "redemption." It not only means redeeming harlots and drunkards and worldly people. It includes acting redemptively to restore church members who have sinned. There is no place in a true church for censoriousness and condemnation. True holiness is winsome as Christ was winsome. Holiness is never more holy than when it reaches out (not down!) to lend a hand of helpfulness and understanding. We have never entered into the spirit of Christ, much less been filled with the Holy Spirit, until we learn to weep with those who weep and tenderly draw them to us and to Him!

The main emotion that is felt in a spiritual community is joy. There is joy in heaven over a sinner who repents, and in the spiritual community as well! But there is more than this. There is joy that comes through enthusiasm. People involved in a crusade get much strength through the joy of their common task. This joy is a rare kind of happiness which the world does not really know. It is the peculiar gift of God to people who are on the march together for Him.

For this reason, a church should always concern itself with morale. Whatever creates disunity destroys joy. With joy, a church can do anything. Without it, little can be done at all. Just try to raise a big budget in a church that is torn by factionalism or which is short of joy!

A true church is an army, not a social club of dilettantes! It grapples with sorrow, but the sorrow is like that of comrades in the battle, not of petty people nursing their bruises.

A true church is strong in doctrine, but it does not teach that a Christian is known only for his correct doctrine. Instead, the true church needs so much of the power of God to make it work that it teaches its members it is the power of God in the life of man that is the true mark of a Christian. The church is thus not only a doctrinal seminary, but a powerhouse.

A spiritual community is an educational institution which educates for a purpose. It does not look on Christian education as an end in itself, or something to be enjoyed as a delightful intellectual pursuit. In the true church "soldiers" are trained to fight, "doctors" are trained to heal, "redeemers" are trained to redeem. For this reason, the true church is centered around Christ the Redeemer, who trains us to follow Him.

The spiritual community is a revolutionary task force of dedicated Christians, not a society for the conservation of obsolete mores. It is a team of ministers and not a club of spiritual pets. Nor is it a debating society. It is Christ's committed action force.

It operates by faith and not by fear. It always tackles more than is possible and more than is reasonable, and succeeds.

The reason that this is often possible is that in any congregation there is more strength, talent, aptitudes, and gifts than have ever been set free! Only in the spiritual community can there be a program which unshackles all this power. In the

The Church as a Spiritual Community

average church there would be no way to harness all the latent power that can potentially be released.

A true church is a high command of strategists who are learning the art of spiritual warfare. They see the enemies of God and are constantly thinking of how to come to grips with them. They rebuke the narrow provincialisms and selfish attitudes of their own wishes and think of the Kingdom of God, the needs of the world, the peril to our freedoms from communism and socialism. They take a long look and see the wider vision of the world, the nation, the times, and plan the church's strategy to go on the offensive.

The true church is a group of stewards who see all things as entrusted to them by God to use for Him. They know that real stewardship is not the church budget only, nor even great offerings for worthy causes, but the regular accounting to God each week of what they have done with all their wealth, including how much they have given to His work.

Will it shock you to know that the spiritual community understands the laws of capitalism and uses them wisely to grow rich? Not, mind you, so that it may be rich and increased with goods and have need of nothing (Revelation 3:17). That God abhors! But growing rich that it might have more to give, more facilities to serve God's people, more to invest in redemption, more to invest in urging attendance so that greater and greater sums might be available to do God's work in the best ways.

The redemptive community's operating costs are not cheap. It *does* too much. But it can do so much because its people believe in it and give sacrificially when they see it rendering such a great service—so many lives being changed, so many real accomplishments. The spiritual community does not fear debt, if the debt is an investment in greater service, increased enlistment of new people, more effective promotion of the work of the church. In a sense, no true church ought to be *out* of debt! This indicates that there are serious failures in its program, for no church can greatly succeed unless it greatly risks.

A church can only practice stewardship if it challenges every member to the limit of his consecration. Stewardship is essentially the awareness that every talent, all our time, and every cent we have is God's. And all is to be used for Him. It is not, as is so often misunderstood, the idea that some of what we have is His. It is all His. And we give all we can to His work, because He gave us what we have for this purpose. He will give us more if we will use more for Him. He will give us as much as we have faith to desire for His glory and are willing to use for His Kingdom. We are people with a trust, a total trust, and all of it is His, on loan to us. The more we are willing to do with His trust for His work, the greater will be the trust. A tithe is only the beginning—the minimum. Faith in God expressed in stewardship carries us far beyond this.

One final thought about the spiritual community: it is a community devoted to devotional and intercessory prayer. It does not operate by human ingenuity or human resources alone. It is a divinely-commissioned group designed to be the agents of God on earth. It must have direct connections with headquarters. It must be concerned for the welfare and deliverance of its members. It must rely upon God through prayer and guidance by the Scriptures for constant correction and improvement of its program. It cannot truly reach *out* in enlistment and service till it first reaches *upward* for strength and guidance.

This, then is the practical application of the theory of the true church—the redemptive, spiritual community.

Nineteen
TRUE AND FALSE CONCEPTS OF EKKLESIA

It is time to discover what is permanent and what is emerging in the church which will change it forever. This is an age of change, and many familiar church ways which we have assumed were permanent are being abandoned or transformed.

Human nature has not changed, but society has; and it is rapidly dissolving around us. New forms and relationships are evolving and are affecting the churches, as they are all other segments of society. We must rediscover what the true church is, and what Christ intended it to be.

It is impossible to define for the general public the institution called "the church." This is a word which is unfortunately now used to describe religion in general; a house of worship; a denomination; Christianity; an assembly of Christians; the family of God; an audience of worshipers; an organization of clergymen and laymen; or simply those who believe in Christ. How can *one* word be used to describe so many things? The answer is that it cannot; it should not be so used. The word *church* denotes primarily the local congregation.

The average Christian thinks of the church in terms of his own congregation, and this is as it should be. But at the same time, we should beware of failing to see the importance of the local congregation in the world strategy of the Kingdom of God. Christian work must be related to churches and church building (not church buildings!).

Another peril is that we may think that the weaknesses or strengths of our own congregation are universal. Still another is that we will not be aware that a true church *can* exist, because we fail to see it in our own church. We may think, therefore, that the true church is unattainable and we can do nothing to help recover it. Lack of vision is one of the sins of Christians today.

Even invalids or others who cannot attend church must *think* of the churches, and endeavor to help establish *true* churches.

How foolish to think of the church, upon which God's strategy depends, only in terms of whether it serves us, interests us, pleases *us*. "Christ also loved the church, and gave himself for it" (Ephesians 5:25). If we love Him, we will do the same. You dare not ignore the church—for in so doing, you weaken the work of God for which Christ died.

Everyone who reads these words should pass them on to others. Especially should ministers read this book. They can do more than others to produce a true church among their own congregations. But if they turn away from the task, deliverance will have to arise from another source.

A revolution is coming. Indeed it is here now. It is a revolution of the spirit, and out of it the world will either be cleansed or a dark age will be born. If the true church can again be vitalized, there will be a bright day for all, and the Antichrist could well be held at bay for another generation.

From the aspect of the methodology or the mechanics of the structure of church organization, it is evident there are numerous ways to successfully build a congregation. There is no single magic method, organization principle, or formula by which to build a church, or to keep a church vital, or to make it strong enough to survive. Churches ebb and flow. In part, this is determined by local conditions, social pressures, traditions, and resources. There are no standard criteria for pronouncing any given church a success. Bigness or wealth is certainly no standard or judgment; small churches often require as much skill to administer as large churches. Though large membership is not a virtue, neither is smallness.

The important thing to remember is that any church should operate at its own capacity of effort and be at its very best—not accepting alibis for its failure, nor excusing its weakness when that weakness is due to lack of diligence.

FORCES WHICH OBSCURE OR DESTROY THE TRUE CHURCH

As an illustration, there is the tragic tendency of evangelists to lose zeal after a time. It is all too evident how many young evangelists slowly forfeit idealism and become security-minded when they suffer ill treatment at the hands of thoughtless congregations. As they age, some become cynical. Others become obsessed with money or power-lust; others retreat into sports, hobbies, or other activities.

In the retreat from a power-anointed, zealous concern for souls, a minister may become interested primarily in his income. He does not, of course, make this transition instantly, but imperceptibly—a small step at a time. Here, a church treats him unfairly; there, he has a long period when there are no calls for his services. So he slowly begins, under family or financial pressures, to armor himself with protection. He works out techniques for making more money, getting more engagements, and paying the political price for publicity or fame. Slowly his power ebbs as his techniques improve. One day he is less a Christian than when he began his ministry—yet unable to realize it. He has become a professional Christian, whose trust is no longer in God. He is perhaps better known, but no longer is he saintly. Like King Saul, he is unaware that the Spirit has departed from him!

But if all this is true about some evangelists, it is also true of the pastor, the denominational worker, the religious bureaucrat. To all of us in the ministry, the voice of God to Jeremiah should be read afresh: "Seekest thou great things for thyself? seek them not: . . . thy life I will give unto thee for a prey in all places whither thou goest" (45:5).

All of this is not to deny the value of the use of methods and techniques. Any "method" will work, provided it is *worked*! But there are men who have surrounded themselves with tricks, promotional schemes, and attendance gimmicks to the neglect of the nature of the true church and the goal of the survival of Christianity.

Ancient churches or long-established denominations are unthinkingly accepted as "true" churches, when they are sometimes no more than spiritual fossils. "I cannot brag about the number of baptisms this year," said a pastor of a very historic Boston church to me at a Harvard Divinity School reunion. "But I *would* like you to see my beautiful marble frescoes." I was tempted to think, "How reminiscent of the Pharisees, who were likened by Christ to sepulchers, beautiful on the outside, but full of coldness and death within!"

New Testament Churches Today: Practical Application

THE ESTABLISHMENT

We hear much about the existence of "the establishment" in American political life. But how about the "establishment" in religious circles? Is it the *true* church? Hardly! It is more often antichurch and prosocialist. For those ministers who work within it, almost any failure is tolerated. But apart from it, no matter the success of purpose or program, ministers are "lesser breeds outside the law." Probably the greatest enemy the true church has is the "establishment," when it tries to undermine the true church by encouraging antichurch policies in the name of the church.

ECUMENICALISM

The panaceas of the past are fast losing relevance for the church in this changing age. Ecumenicalism seeks growth through uniting that which already exists. The very thirst for ecumenicalism is often a sign of decadence. Those religious bodies seeking to unite are usually not evangelizing effectively. They are like dying corporations which seek to cover their retreat by amalgamation and the resultant illusion of temporal and temporary power. The idealism of a united Christian front is frequently merely the rationalizing of a fear of decline. The cults which plague Christianity have at least this virtue—they are conquering, not compromising with others as fearful as themselves. A proselytizing zeal may not be true evangelism, but it is better than a closing of ranks to cover retreat.

WORLDLY COMPETITION

Competition for the interest and affection of people is the keenest it has ever been in the history of Christianity. Never has the world been more attractive and distractive. For every temptation our fathers had, we have ten. For every distraction they knew, we face a hundred. The commercialism of pleasure and recreation; the ease of transportation to whisk us out of reach of the church; for the teenager, the ill-placed emphasis upon the high school as the supreme arbiter of taste, morals, social life, and recreation, instead of mere education which is its only proper role; the affluence of our society with two houses, two cars, more leisure time, and more money to spend on luxuries—all this convinces most people that this is the best of all possible worlds and that they do not "need" God.

True and False Concepts of Ekklesia

This affluence has resulted in a corresponding decline in moral and spiritual discipline. Never has it been so easy and respectable to avoid the will of God. And all of this constitutes reasons for the decline of the local church. We can expect it to continue and not abate. Only a national calamity or a revival of the divine plan for the church will prevent the eventual decline and fall of many of our contemporary churches.

Unless the church (in the local, immediate sense) examines its premise, its reason for being, it will most surely go into decline. The decline is now upon us and will become epidemic unless we examine the role of the church in the mind of Christ and the Apostles.

Another threat to the church is the multiplication of non-church "Christian" activity, which is a kind of revolution against the church. It is sadly true that when the church neglects a good doctrine, the cults will seize upon it (and probably pervert it). It is also true that when the church neglects its mission, there are independent forces which will take it over, with a range of results from good to bad—and to the dismay or even the damage of the church itself.

In any age, and more particularly in our own, the church that is truly the church, that which can survive the century and keep the Faith on earth in purity and reality, will be and has been marked by certain essentials, the neglect of any one of which is fatal. This study has been made to force us to reconsider those essentials.

PARTIAL ANSWERS TO OUR DILEMMA

There is no magic button we can press which will set all things right. There are many solutions, all of which have constructive values. Here are some:

EVANGELISM

Some evangelism is not as effective as it once was. Much "modern evangelism" is getting tiresome and is being rejected. But no biblically oriented Christian should neglect evangelism, since it is a command of Christ. There has been a wholesome resurgence of mass evangelism; and this is sorely needed to make a massive impact upon the general public. But some church evangelism, in terms of the dull, routine, twice-a-year revival conducted with regularity in the average church, is fast losing relevancy and is being abandoned.

Alas! No effective substitute has been found. Visitation evangelism was in vogue for a time, as were other attempts, such as youth evangelism, open-air services, tract distribution, and noonday services. But these were only methods of evangelism and had no permanence inherent in them. Some of these methods and others will continue, but they are by no means universally effective.

THE HOLY SPIRIT MOVEMENT

At present, there is a thrust toward the effective promotion of vitality in the Christian message by a proliferation of the healing movement, and the experience of the Holy Spirit, even in churches which hitherto have shied away from these miraculous experiences. This is to say that Pentecostalism has leaped over the wall of separation between the tabernacles and store-building churches and the more traditional churches. This at least removes an unnecessary barricade in the Christian family, and makes it more popular for churchmen to believe once more in the living Christ, the power of the Holy Spirit, and the possibility of a genuine experience of God.

Though sooner or later a reaction to this may set in, this new thrust might well help postpone the decadence of some of the churches for another generation, and for this we may be grateful. The problem shall be to translate this revival into permanence for those to whom it has relevance. The danger is that this charismatic movement may become, as it has in some churches, divisive. If an emphasis upon the Holy Spirit is genuine, the experience should result in the fruits of the Spirit!

RESEARCH IN THE CHURCHES

One of the great problems of churches seeking to be true churches and seeking to anticipate what is enduring in Christianity is that there is little research, such as business firms constantly conduct, being done into the question of survival. Most pastors are too busy with their own immediate problems to bother with asking the big questions. Denominational officials are sometimes even less creative, since they are often mostly concerned with their own security and the prosperity of their own provincial bureaucracy. Indeed, creative men don't frequently achieve denominational posts, which instead are awarded to those who cooperate and conform, rather than to those who question redemptively the axiom of tradition.

But research into better methods in the church can offer a hopeful signpost toward more effectiveness, whatever the source. It would be hoped that seminaries and graduate schools of theology will help to pioneer research for the churches. Local churches which are innovative also are promising sources of new ideas. Above all, we need to recover an insight into what the true church should be.

Remarkable stone and marble remnants of an idol and grave markers from the time of St. Paul, in Berea, Greece.

Twenty

BIBLICAL BASES
OF THE TRUE CHURCH

Too long have we lacked the clear vision that whatever else the concept "church" means, it mostly means the "people," clergy and laity alike! We have suffered enough from the notion that the clergy should be a class apart. To millions, the laity is considered as an audience before whom the clergy performs. We are as much victims of being spectators in religion as we are in sports. Our task is to get people out of the stands and onto the fields! We must convince them that all church members are the team.

Elton Trueblood has suggested that we too often think of the congregation as an orchestral society before whom the orchestra (clergy and choirs) perform. Between performances (Sundays) the society may relax, for the responsibilities lie with those on the platform. Dr. Trueblood urges that Christians realize instead that in reality they are the orchestra, not the orchestral society! In the Christian pattern there is a recognizable division of labor, and there will be a conductor, but all should perform. In the final sense, the audience of a worship service is not the congregation, but God!

Whatever moves the pastor away from the people in worship is a dishonor to the symbolism of the pulpit. One cannot conceive of Jesus willingly associating Himself with any such thing. God thrust Himself amidst mankind in Christ. The throne was vacant in favor of the marketplace, the synagogue, the seashore, and the throngs on the hillsides and in the busy streets. Our Lord was a layman!

Our task is to rediscover a way by which all Christians, lay and clerical, may see themselves as ministers of Jesus Christ. If this idea would be taken seriously by our people, we would find ourselves with a spiritual revolution on our hands. As Dr. True-

New Testament Churches Today: Practical Application

blood observes, the number of ministers in the average church would change from only one to *hundreds*! In the early church, "the non-ministering member was nonexistent!"

In a real sense, church membership is a kind of ordination. By it, a person is accepted for the Christian ministry. All true members of the church are, or should be, ministers. Some are designated to preach, some to teach, some to serve tables, some to counsel, some to heal. But all are ministers. Some give all their time; others can give only a portion to the church and must minister through their secular positions as well. For most of his career St. Paul was a minister of this latter kind. He seldom was paid by the churches, but was he any less a minister because of it?

The pastor's function is to remind the church that they, as well as he, are ministers of the church. St. Paul urged laymen as well as pastors to conduct themselves so that "the ministry be not blamed" (2 Corinthians 6:3).

The doctrine of the priesthood of all believers means more than unhampered access to God by all Christians. It means that *all* Christians are priests, for themselves *and for others*. Christ, the great High Priest, recognizes a universal priesthood of intercession, not of mediation. Paul says: "Now then we are ambassadors for Christ, as though God did beseech you by us: we pray you in Christ's stead, be ye reconciled to God" (2 Corinthians 5:20).

The hope for the future lies in an awakened awareness of the total responsibility of the church for the ministry. This concept of all Christians as ministers has been obscured, but its roots are firmly implanted in the New Testament. What kind of contemporary church must we become in order to preserve this idea? The answer is plain. The church must be the product of much wider participation by all its ministers (i.e., people) than is now commonly practiced. The church must be a "spiritual community."

It would seem that we are now engaged in a contest to see whether the church can, in fact, endure. There are those who mistakenly believe an "audience-preacher type" of church is sufficient. But others of us believe the future belongs only to the "spiritual-community type" of church, where every member is a minister. We will not have long to wait to see which will prevail, for one or the other will not survive. But can we afford to wait?

154

Biblical Bases of the True Church

The "redemptive-community" kind of church is the hope of the future, in the opinion of many. But it must be understood as an idea or concept before its benefits can be realized.

The word "community" normally means a group of people who reside in the same area with a center of government, business, and public service which draws them together in common interests. A town or neighborhood is a type of "civic" or "secular" community. Even though it may have churches in it, it is primarily a secular community.

There are also "religious" communities such as monasteries or settlements of people of common religious backgrounds (e.g., the Doukhobors of Canada, or the Dunkards of Pennsylvania). These colonies, however, are still civic communities with an ecclesiastical or church government, or at least with a religious center of interest.

The "spiritual community" is radically different from either the civic or the religious community. It is always a church or congregation of people. But it is a church that makes religion a way of life, seven days a week, rather than a compartment of life limited to religious activities on Sunday morning. It is more than simply a Sunday school and worship service. It is a redeeming spiritual force within the secular community.

It is most of all a kind of church that makes of its people a *family* because of shared relationship by the "new birth" and resulting new interests in spiritual matters. (We call it a *community* rather than a *family* because churches are usually so large that they resemble communities rather than families.)

When a person is regenerated, God becomes his Father and he becomes God's child. Other Christians also have become children of God. There is therefore a "blood" relationship between all Christians that makes "twice born" people actual brothers and sisters in the family of those who call the same God "Father." This family relationship is the only true basis of the spiritual family or community. The spiritual community without the spiritual family cannot succeed, for then it is not based upon a divine relationship.

In the redemptive-community type of church there is, as its second qualification, a very deep consecration to God, Christ, and the things of the Spirit. Its members, for the most part, have decided that spiritually motivated living is the most important thing in the world. Because of this they come regularly to the worship services. A great deal of their social activity centers around the church. Their intimate friendships are largely (though perhaps not exclusively) among fellow church members, and more and more they find that they have little in common with those who are not spiritually like-minded.

If these people need counseling, they turn to the churches and their ministers or leaders. If they need help, they find their church eager to stand by them. When old age or death comes, their fellow church members as members of the same spiritual family are best able to comfort and assure them. In poverty or depression, the church shares with its people, so that in emergencies they may look to the church instead of the state.

It is obvious that many churches are already spiritual families or communities to some degree. The concern of this plea is that they *realize* this and see clearly the path they should take to deepen and widen their program, until all churches are consciously working toward being full-pledged spiritual communities whose mission is total redemption.

When this basic spiritual family is established, with true spiritual interest as the motivating factor that draws people into this new family relationship, then the family will find ways of extending its services to its family to take better care of it, and to serve it more widely and effectively.

There are some churches which mistakenly think they can solve their problems by adding a youth program or building a recreation building. Nothing could be further from the truth. Such a church is in for disillusionment. Churches can be true spiritual families or communities *without any buildings at all.* Buildings and large well-trained staffs of leaders are very helpful, but these things are the result of the spiritual community, not the cause of it.

This is precisely the way the redemptive community works: People are attracted by the message of the cross to the spiritual family. The family, seeing itself not as an audience but as a community, then serves its corporate members in the multiple ways their needs and its resources indicate. Through the years, it adds to its program and buildings and eventually becomes a veritable spiritual "city of God" with scores of organizations, constantly meeting and working, to bring the richness of the *total Gospel* to the total needs of its members.

To see the church as a congregation or corporation is not so much wrong as inadequate! There are more dimensions to it than that. The New Testament church was a closely knit family in the heart of each Roman town. It was a redemptive community that stressed spiritual relationship. First, it related men to God as "children," and second, to each other as "brothers." The early church did not think of humanity at large as brothers, but rather looked only upon members of the church as brothers and sisters. It considered those outside of the church as *fellow creatures*, who knew God only as Creator and who needed to be won to a new relation of sonship with God, and who then would become "brethren" as members of the new family.

All the program of the New Testament church flowed out of this spiritual relationship. Unless the church, any church, follows this order, consciously or unconsciously, it is missing the purpose of Christ for His church, and too, the most potent source of power, strong enough to resist all deterioration and competition.

The church as a redemptive community frankly asks to be the center of the activities of the Christian family, second only to the home. It is the object of sacrificial stewardship. It provides the widest and most wholesome social relationships. It teaches the family, by many means, to become "God conscious" in all their activities. It sets a standard of moral values and gives help to the family to live by that standard. It counsels the family in distress and provides outlets for service for all who seek to work for God and good causes. It inspires and directs its people to go out into the civic community and be a redemptive influence in the name of Christ. It seeks to persuade and teach, by doctrine and example, that the business of the Christian church is to bind up the bleeding wounds of humanity, not to make those wounds greater. While it realizes that there will always be those who reject Christ and the church, it never stops trying to win as many as possible to active discipleship.

Above all, it is not an exclusive organization which holds itself above the civic community, frostily excluding all who do not belong. It is, rather, an inclusive agency, always endeavoring to win all who can be persuaded to seek fellowship and membership in the family of God. It exists not to judge, but to redeem. This is what makes it irresistibly attractive.

The redemptive community is only possible if the people are first of all spiritual. One might even say, the physical things of the church are at best possible tools or facilities. All of them can be sacrificed without total loss. *The core concept of the church is an idea or attitude*. How the idea expresses itself in a staff, or a program, or in a building, parish hall, gymnasium, or a special youth recreation program is entirely up to the local congregation. But a marvelous transformation can take place in both the people and the spiritual community. New bonds of unity, harmony, and teamwork can be forged. New redemptive attitudes can begin to exert their glorious lifting spirit. The whole atmosphere of a church can be changed overnight. This frequently happened in the early church.

THE THEOLOGICAL BASIS OF THE REDEMPTIVE COMMUNITY

The main biblical idea of the church was, from the beginning, the concept of a continuing congregation in full organized fellowship—a colony of God's people in, but not of, the secular community—the city of God within the city of man. Augustine's idea of "The City of God" was that the "catholic church" would take the place of the state and govern the whole of life. The idea of the spiritual community is sharply antagonistic to that of Augustine and completely different from it.

The idea of community has been integral to the life and thought and concept of the churches ever since the first believers were aware of being a very special *koinonia* (fellowship). The Christian concept of the church as a redemptive community stands over against all other concepts of community as a judgment upon them, and as a condemnation of their efforts to find fellowship other than in the fullest Christian terms. It is tragic that this concept of the church is today only one of several competing concepts of the church. The whole point of this appeal is to get churches to return to the original concept as the best, if not the only, workable concept of the local church.

158

Biblical Bases of the True Church

Many Christian leaders, of great insight, stress the essential community nature of the primitive congregation. Dr. Gaines S. Dobbins (*Building Better Churches*) says:

> Christianity introduced the concept of "the beloved community." In this concept the community consists of like-minded people bound together by ties of common experience, common purpose, common faith, common love. The community thus conceived breaks over barriers of class and race, and takes on world-wide dimensions.

Dr. John Mackay of Princeton described the thrust of mission field churches back toward the New Testament idea:

> In those countries, the church becomes the total environment of the Christian's life, rather than one among the circles in which he moves.
>
> The sense of the church and its centrality in the Christian religion had been to a large extent dead and needed to be reborn.
>
> The church in the sense in which it is used in this letter is not primarily an organization or an institution but a community. It is the community of those for whom Jesus Christ is Lord.

Dr. Emil Brunner says:

> The act of becoming a believer ... is the event in which a human being becomes conscious of community, the act by which he abandons forever all solitary detached existence. The Holy Spirit is calling in order to create his community.

Willis Lamott adds, in *Revolution in Missions*:

> Experience on the mission field has demonstrated that the gospel is commended to unbelievers by the corporate witness of the new life as lived within the

fellowship as a "colony of heaven," a cross-section of the kingdom to come where new relations are set up that amaze and attract outsiders, as much as by the witness of the individual evangelist.... The Church as fellowship is not only the end of evangelism; it is the agent in that process.

Dr. John D. Smart (*The Teaching Ministry of the Church*) stresses the fellowship aspect of the spiritual community:

We have only to describe the fellowship of the early church to be made aware of the deficiency of the modern congregation.

It is the shame of the Church that there are so many congregations where a stranger can enter and leave without ever being made aware of the existence of any fellowship. This is nothing less than a failure of the church to be the church; it has become a conglomeration of individuals rather than a close-knit fellowship.

Dr. George Laird Hunt (*Rediscovering the Church*) describes the events which have forced attention on the concept of the spiritual community:

It is time now to ask what it is that men are seeking in the midst of the social change which history has forced upon us. It is no new thing. It is the same thing that man has sought from the beginning of time. Each period of history simply puts the search in a new context and surrounds it with new props and problems. It is the search for personal significance.

The search involves relationship to other people.

What we are searching for is community. Community is found in any relationship where the personality of each person within it is respected, where no one person tries to dominate anyone else, where each person can speak his mind freely, where each feels

160

that the truth spoken to him by another person is uttered in respect and love and not for any impure motive. It is a relationship of harmony and peace.

This relationship is found within the church. Here men are always nonconformists, for their only allegiance forces them to be against the conformists that are contrary to His will. But here men accept one another freely, for here men know themselves as persons united to one another by their reconciliation through the atoning sacrifice of Jesus Christ.

Dr. Roy Burkhart (*How The Church Grows*) speaks of the spiritual community concept as "the true church."

Whenever there is a beloved community of those who seek together the whole truth and live it in love, there also is the True Church. It is a church of, by and for those who make it up, constantly sensitive both to the Holy Spirit and to the needs of men locally and over the world. It seeks not to bring the neighborhood within its four walls, but to create the beloved community in the neighborhood. It loses itself in ministry to the spiritual needs of all, and the heart of its ministry is to free men and to keep them free to seek the Kingdom of God.

Australian evangelist Alan Walker, an internationally known Methodist, in a sermon at the Riverside Church, New York, commented:

Jesus Christ has given to us the community of Christians called the church. The church as a fact is part of the face of Christ, part of the essential contribution Jesus Christ makes to man. It is significant that in the early chapters of the Book of Acts, Christians, before they were called by that proud title, were known as the "People of the Way," a new community of people. And so, as people watched this new community of people move through the world, they said: "Ha, People of the Way." And it was precisely because these "People of the Way" took their historic journey through the earth that the ancient world of Greece and Rome was arrested. And precisely because there was a new community of people that emerged, a new culture, the Christian culture, came into being.

Over in Australia, or in any country where your country is represented, we have a little bit of American territory. Right at the heart of Canberra, their national capital, there is the American Embassy. And if, as an American citizen, you step on that piece of soil, the laws of Australia do not operate. You are under the President of the United States. And we, if we are obedient to Jesus Christ, are set down in a colony of heaven, where the laws of heaven operate.

I have quoted at great length from various authorities, of differing denominational backgrounds, to demonstrate that the concept of the church as a spiritual community (rather than a mere audience or congregation) is not new, but the authentic position of thoughtful Christian leaders everywhere.

THE BIBLICAL FOUNDATION OF THE REDEMPTIVE COMMUNITY

Most well-read Christian ministers today are aware of the pitfalls of the proof text method of biblical exegesis. Theology must be based upon the whole teaching of the Scriptures as well as upon isolated passages. In this section we shall merely attempt to list the widespread descriptions of the spiritual community in the New Testament.

The phrase "spiritual community" does not appear as such. Yet it is quite biblical, in that it is the closest we can come to a verbal description of what the New Testament assembly was actually like.

The church was not described nor defined objectively as a "redemptive community," probably because it was already so obvi-

Biblical Bases of the True Church

ous to the people who first read the books of the New Testament that they simply took it for granted. We must remember that the churches were in existence long before the Epistles and Gospels were written.

Yet it must not be supposed that the idea of the redemptive community is based only upon inference. On the contrary, the theme of the redemptive community sweeps through the New Testament as an underlying concept. Look then at the functions of the church as described in the New Testament.

Disputes between Christians in matters of property or personal rights were considered under the jurisdiction of the spiritual community.

> Dare any of you, having a matter against another, go to law before the unjust, and not before the saints? Do ye not know that the saints shall judge the world? and if the world shall be judged by you, are ye unworthy to judge the smallest matters? (1 Corinthians 6:1, 2).
>
> But if he will not hear thee, then take with thee one or two more, that in the mouth of two or three witnesses every word may be established. And if he shall neglect to hear them, *tell it unto the church*: but if he neglect to hear the church, let him be unto thee as an heathen man and a publican (Matthew 18:16, 17).

It was a church that had a multi-sided program which covered many aspects of life besides the strictly religious. This is obvious from the descriptions given of the various types of ministries in the early church.

> And God hath set some in the church, first apostles, secondarily prophets, thirdly teachers, after that miracles, then gifts of healings, helps, governments, diversities of tongues (1 Corinthians 12:28).

The church was centered in both the house of worship and in the homes of the people. It was not dependent upon buildings or facilities, but was found wherever people congregated.

> I kept back nothing that was profitable unto you, but have showed you, and have taught you *publicly*, and *from house to house* (Acts 20:20).
>
> And daily in the *temple*, and *in every house*, they ceased not to teach and preach Jesus Christ (Acts 5:42).
>
> And they, continuing daily with one accord in the *temple*, and breaking bread *from house to house*, did eat their meat with gladness and singleness of heart (Acts 2:46).

It was a program of fellowship with all that may imply. Fellowship, so strangely missing in our "audience concept" churches, was a vital part of the New Testament assembly.

> And they continued steadfastly in the apostles' doctrine and *fellowship*, and in *breaking of bread*, and in prayers (Acts 2:42).

The church was an evangelizing community which functioned seven days a week, always busy redeeming people.

> And they, *continuing daily* with one accord in the temple, and breaking bread from house to house, did eat their meat with gladness and singleness of heart. Praising God, and having favor with all the people. And the Lord added to the church *daily* such as should be saved (Acts 2:46, 47).
>
> And *daily* in the temple, and in every house, they ceased not to teach and preach Jesus Christ (Acts 5:42).
>
> And so were the churches established in the faith, and increased in number *daily* (Acts 16:5).
>
> But when divers were hardened, and believed not, but spake evil of that way before the multitude, he departed from them, and separated the disciples, disputing *daily* in the school of one Tyrannus (Acts 19:9).

Biblical Bases of the True Church

The church sponsored a program of healing of body and mind. A careful study of healing in the New Testament church will reveal that it was much wider than the realm of the physical. Wholeness was sought more than mere physical healing. Mental, emotional, physical, and spiritual needs were thought of as connected. Redemption was available for all.

> Insomuch that they brought forth the sick into the streets, and laid them on beds and couches, that at the least the shadow of Peter passing by might overshadow some of them (Acts 5:15).
>
> And God wrought special miracles by the hands of Paul: So that from his body were brought unto the sick handkerchiefs or aprons, and the diseases departed from them, and the evil spirits went out of them (Acts 19:11, 12).

This was the New Testament church. A redemptive, spiritual community where fellow believers in the Lord Jesus Christ came together to worship God and build up one another in their mutual faith. They were an assembly devoted to their Savior and to each other. They were indeed a community joined together by Christ.

Thus we should be today.